LAWRENCE DALLAGLIO

My Italian Family
COOKBOOK
recipes from three generations

SIMON &
SCHUSTER
ILLUSTRATED

London · New York · Sydney · Toronto

A CBS COMPANY

LAWRENCE DALLAGLIO

My Italian Family
COOKBOOK
recipes from three generations

To Vincenzo, Alice, Ella, Josie and Enzo,
not forgetting my dear sister Francesca
and my mother Eileen, who have all been,
and continue to be, my inspiration.

Powerful together.

First published in Great Britain
by Simon & Schuster UK Ltd, 2011
A CBS COMPANY

1 3 5 7 9 10 8 6 4 2

SIMON & SCHUSTER
ILLUSTRATED BOOKS
Simon & Schuster UK Ltd
222 Gray's Inn Road
London
WC1X 8HB

www.simonandschuster.co.uk

Simon & Schuster Australia
Sydney

A CIP catalogue record for this book is available from the British Library

ISBN 978-0-85720-271-0
ISBN 978-0-85720-562-9 (corporate edition)

Editorial director: Francine Lawrence
Project editor: Hilary Ivory
Design: XAB Design
Photography: Ruth Jenkinson and Steve Baxter
Home economy: Emma Marsden
Production manager: Katherine Thornton
Commercial director: Ami Richards

Colour reproduction by Dot Gradations Ltd, UK
Printed and bound in China

My Italian Family COOKBOOK

what my father taught me...

I've been passionate about food from as far back as I can remember. Not just eating it, but all the sensory rituals that go with it: tracking down the best ingredients; the chopping, stirring, sizzling, hissing; the aroma of Bolognese bubbling on the hob. Smell can, in an instant, send me hurtling back in time to warm summer holidays spent in my grandmother's kitchen in Italy.

My dad, Vincenzo, a native of Turin and the embodiment of all things Italian – fine food, good wine and Juventus – spent a lifetime in the food business. Starting off at the Lido in Venice, he climbed the ladder via top-class hotels across the world before arriving at the London Metropole. Am I the only boy who, at age 12, enjoyed a six-month stay in the Westminster Suite at the top of the Metropole? My parents were house-hunting at the time and, looking back on it, this was probably where my love of good food started. There can't have been many youngsters in England who breakfasted on smoked salmon and scrambled eggs, then went to school with croissants for the boys at break. If that was kick-off most mornings, close of play was equally impressive, usually spent in the grill room dining on lemon sole or sea bass. It was a hell of a way for a boy to educate his palate.

Just as unusually for that era, when he wasn't tied up at work Dad did a lot of the cooking. Nowadays I tell Enzo, my 10-year-old, that if he can't cook he needn't expect to achieve babe-magnet status – it's definitely a skill that adds a certain something to a guy's social life. In fact, being able to cook was one of the few things that impressed Alice, now my wife! At his age, I vividly remember the admiration of friends who would drop by and, as always in our house, chat at the kitchen table while my father prepared a meal. They'd be stunned at his care and precision – everyday cooking elevated to an art form.

My summer holidays, usually spent with my grandparents, who ran a stall in Turin's fruit and vegetable market, also revolved around food. Shopping for ingredients in Italy is a national obsession. The market square is without doubt the hub of social activity. The same scrutinising of fruit and vegetables goes on today as it has done for centuries. Ingredients are discussed and produce picked over until just the right degree of ripeness is found. I discovered this early, when I was allowed to help on the stall, a coveted opportunity to enter the baffling world of grown-ups. It was an important lesson in the first rule of cooking: always start with fresh, top-quality ingredients.

That was then, but it has very much shaped the realisation of a dream long nurtured by my father and me: to take our passion for good food a stage further and market our own sauces. For Vincenzo, with his excellent cooking skills and understanding of good dining, it's important to keep alive old family recipes and see the Dallaglio culinary secrets safely passed on.

I learned my love of cooking from him, picking up techniques while sitting on the kitchen counter, seeing how to follow a recipe, tasting and adjusting flavours. Now the baton has been passed to me, and it's my turn to show Enzo, Ella and Josie that cooking with great ingredients is fun, and doing it as a family even more so.

---

top left 1995: playing for the England A team.
top right 1980: St Osmunds School photo of me with my sister, Francesca.
middle left Asti, May 2009: lunch with (from left) Lorenzo Ercole (President of Sacla'), me, his daughter Chiara (granddaughter of the founders) and Vincenzo.
middle right September 2009: with Caldicott School boys at a training session, followed by a lunch of pasta and new sauces to celebrate their launch.
bottom left Barnes, London, September 1968: the wedding of my parents, Vincenzo and Eileen.
bottom right Provence, 1988: on holiday with Alice and our eldest daughter, Ella.

Me, aged eight, with my sister Francesca, who tragically died in the sinking of the *Marchioness* on the Thames in 1989. It's the memory of my mother's tireless efforts to get justice for my sister and all the young lives lost on that boat that inspired me to start the Dallaglio Foundation. Our slogan is 'Powerful together', and it does what it says, drawing groups and communities together to work to raise money and provide opportunities for people less fortunate than I am.

Powerful together

Dallaglio Foundation

www.dallagliofoundation.com

There is unquestionable truth in the saying 'You are what you eat'. I believe that my robust good health and ability to withstand the gruelling training regimes and massive energy requirements of playing rugby at world level have been due, in large part, to my excellent diet. That's how the Dallaglio sauces and our slow-baked tomato antipasti came about. My dad and I worked shoulder to shoulder with the Ercole family, owners of Sacla', to produce big-flavoured, big-hearted and health-promoting sauces.

Putting Italian cooking's legendary freshness at the heart of my own growing children's diet is a no-brainer. It's simple, because good ingredients stand best on their own; it's healthy because it's clean and unadulterated. Think about the ingredients that form the backbone of the Italian kitchen and you can see why it's so highly regarded by the medical fraternity worldwide: olive oil, tomatoes, lemons, celery, olives, artichokes, peppers, balsamic vinegar, rice, pasta, polenta, pizza and olive oil breads. The heaviest foods, such as meat, are served last, so it's difficult to over-eat because you haven't any room left. Meals are turned into an event to be shared with family and friends – you chew, talk, chew and talk long into the evening. These principles apply to all good cooking and they underpin the recipes in this book, as well as every single product produced by Sacla'.

Little did we know that when my father and I set out to find the food producer best suited to help us get our ideas to market, our ambition would bring with it the chance to forge the perfect partnership between two Italian families. This relationship has come to have special meaning, because we have such an extraordinary amount in common: our Piedmontese background, a great love of cooking, a passion for the highest quality ingredients, excellent wine, and a deep and abiding love of family and tradition. You only have to sit back and watch Lorenzo Ercole and my dad in the development kitchen in Asti, north-west Italy, or listen to them debating the merits of this tomato or that basil at one of the many joint family lunches, to feel the passion and commitment that has gone into our sauces. It's rare to hook up with people whose values and principles so uncannily mirror your own.

Sacla's success story is heartwarming and it happened for all the right reasons. For us, the fact that it has been owned and run by the same family since it started in 1939, rather than by a faceless, multinational corporation, is hugely important. What's more, the Ercoles come from the same region of Italy, so we have a lot in common. You just get massively more pride, passion and authority from a business whose products are personally controlled by the individuals who own it. We like their spiritedness, their up-for-it attitude and their creative blend of traditional ways with progressive methods. We especially like their ethics – from the way they treat farmers as partners and respect the rhythm of the seasons, to ensuring the lightest possible footprint on the earth and harnessing natural energy to run their operation. Proof of how seriously they take this is that one of their two production sites in Piedmont is powered entirely by the sun. And while we're talking inventive engineering, how many of us know that it was Sacla' who developed the technology to remove the stones from olives? Every time I open a jar of pitted olives I heave a sigh of gratitude.

We care passionately about food, the way it's grown and harvested for our consumption, and the way we cook it. We very much hope that you do, too, and that these recipes will give you and your family as much pleasure as they have given ours, over so many generations.

Finally, I must thank my father Vincenzo, my wife Alice, my children Ella, Josie and Enzo; and the Sacla' family in Italy for their help and support in making this book.

---

top Sydney, 2003: Rugby World Cup final, on the charge in the build-up to Jason Robinson's try.
middle left 1998: playing for Wasps against Gloucester at a very muddy Kingsholm.
middle centre St James's Palace, 2004: with Alice after receiving my MBE from the Queen.
middle right Asti, 2009: Vincenzo shares a joke with Lorenzo Ercole, President of Sacla'.
bottom left Lake Como, 2006: our wedding.
bottom right Asti, 2009: tasting and testing in the development kitchens.

spuntini
light bites

Like yours, my life is hectic. But I've learned that it's
when you're flat out that you can't afford to let your
diet slide. Here are a few nifty ways of getting the
fuel you need without a huge hassle.

fonduta piemontese
fontina cheese fondue

Dad jokes that the Italians invented fondue, not the French. Whatever the truth, this is a family favourite. If you can't get hold of fontina cheese, use mature Cheddar.

Prep time: 5 mins
Cooking time: 5 mins

SERVES 4

INGREDIENTS

300g fontina cheese, chopped
100ml full-fat milk
15g butter
1 tsp plain flour
100ml dry white wine
salt and freshly ground white pepper,
     to season
cubes of bread, toasted

Put the cheese in a bowl and pour over the milk. Leave to soak for a few hours.

Melt the butter in a pan. Stir in the flour and cook for 1 min. Add the milk and cheese and slowly stir everything together.

Pour in the wine, season and simmer for a few minutes. Pour into a fondue dish to keep warm, then serve and let everyone help themselves to the cubes of bread for dipping.

bagna cauda
piedmontese fondue

This recipe takes me back to the rip-roaring, six-hour lunch with the Ercole family at my house to celebrate Dallaglio sauces' first anniversary. *Bagna cauda* happens to be a speciality of Fernanda Ercole, wife of the President of Sacla', so she brought her own recipe over from Italy. It was amazing, but since there's no way she'll divulge hers, you'll have to make do with mine! It's rich and warming, so a little goes a long way.

Prep time: 15 mins
Cooking time: around 20 mins

SERVES 8

INGREDIENTS

2 small garlic cloves, peeled
75ml milk
100g jar anchovies in oil, drained
100ml olive oil
25g unsalted butter, cubed, at room temperature
freshly ground black pepper

For dipping

A selection of raw vegetables: peppers, quartered and deseeded; fennel, outer leaves removed and quartered; celery hearts, quartered; chicory or radicchio, quartered; carrots, peeled and halved lengthways; slices of ciabatta or Italian Pugliese bread

Put the garlic cloves in a small pan with the milk and simmer for 15 mins until soft. Set aside to cool a little.

Place the garlic and the milk in a small blender and whiz to a purée. Add the anchovies next and blend to a thick paste.

Slowly add the oil, dripping it in little by little, as you do when making mayonnaise, making sure that each batch is absorbed before adding the next.

Finally, add the butter, cube by cube, to make a thick, creamy consistency. Season with pepper.

Transfer the *bagna cauda* to a small saucepan to gently warm through – don't let it boil. Stir constantly. Serve with the prepared raw vegetables and lots of bread for dipping.

'This is a real Piedmontese crowd pleaser — serve it up when you've a lot of mouths to feed'

peperoni alla piemontese
marinated peppers with anchovies, garlic and oil

This is one of my favourite ways of cooking peppers – I make it by the bucketload, so there's always some in the fridge for healthy snacking.

Prep time: 15 mins
Cooking time: 20 mins, plus
     marinating time

SERVES 4

INGREDIENTS

3 red or yellow peppers
2 tbsp olive oil
1 garlic clove, peeled and sliced
4 anchovies in oil, drained
1 tbsp capers
salt and freshly ground black pepper

Preheat the grill. Halve the peppers, cut out the core and get rid of the seeds. Place them on a baking sheet skin-side up and grill until blackened all over and the skin starts to peel away.

Tip into an airtight container and seal with the lid. Leave for about 30 mins: the heat from the peppers steams up the container and will make the skin come off more easily.

Peel the peppers and put them in a shallow dish with their juices. Discard the papery skins.

Heat the oil in a small pan with the garlic until you can just begin to smell it. Don't cook it for too long – you don't want it to turn golden, you just want the garlic to release its flavour into the oil.

Pour over the peppers, then snip over the anchovies and scatter over the capers. Season well and toss the ingredients together. Leave to marinate in the fridge for at least 1 hour and up to 24 hours. Make sure you take them out of the fridge around 30 mins before you want to eat them to allow the flavours to develop.

pomodori gratinati
baked tomatoes with breadcrumbs

If you've a glut of tomatoes from your garden, or some that aren't as ripe as they could be, do what the Italians do. Roasting them intensifies the flavour, and when you add garlic and herbs, you make this into a simple starter or easy light lunch.

Prep time: 15 mins
Cooking time: 30–35 mins

SERVES 4

INGREDIENTS

1 slice white bread
4 beef tomatoes, halved horizontally
1–2 tbsp olive oil
1 garlic clove, peeled and crushed
salt and freshly ground black pepper
1 tsp each finely chopped oregano
  and thyme
15g pecorino cheese, freshly grated

Preheat the oven to 200°C/180°C fan oven/gas mark 6.

Chop the bread and put in a small food processor and whiz to make breadcrumbs.

Use a teaspoon to scoop out and discard the seeds from the tomatoes. Put the tomatoes, cut-side up, in a shallow ovenproof dish. Mix together the oil and garlic and season well. Drizzle equally over the tomatoes, making sure the garlic drops into the cavities in the tomatoes.

Mix together the breadcrumbs, herbs and cheese, and season. Sprinkle over the tomatoes and bake in the oven for 30–35 mins until the breadcrumbs start to turn golden and the tomatoes are cooked.

focaccia
italian olive oil bread

This is a typical Italian bread – it's made with more olive oil than you'd normally use in a loaf, but this is what gives it its fantastic moisture.

Prep time: 1 hour 25 mins, including proving time
Cooking time: 30 mins

SERVES 6

INGREDIENTS
25g fresh yeast
500g strong plain flour
1½ tsp salt
3 tbsp olive oil
6 Dallaglio by Sacla' Italian Slow-Baked Tomatoes Marinated With Chilli, chopped, plus some oil from the jar
leaves from a few sprigs of thyme

Put the yeast in 300ml lukewarm water and stir to dissolve. Sift the flour into a large bowl and stir in the salt.

Make a well in the centre and add the olive oil, then pour in the yeast mixture. Stir using a knife, then get stuck in with your hands and knead until the mixture comes together. Put the dough on a board and knead for another 5 mins until smooth and elastic. Don't add more flour – it should be soft and sticky. Put the dough back in a clean bowl, cover and leave for about 45 mins until it has doubled in size.

Dust a board with flour and roll out the dough to make a rectangle of about 30 x 20cm. Line a baking sheet with baking parchment and slide the dough onto it. Leave it in a warm place for about 30 mins to prove – it's ready when you touch it and the soft, pillowy dough springs back.

Now preheat the oven to 200°C/180°C fan oven/gas mark 6. With your fingers, make indents all over the surface. Drizzle with a little chilli oil from the jar, then bake for 20 mins.

Remove from the oven and spoon the chopped oven-baked tomatoes evenly over the bread. Sprinkle over the thyme. Bake for a further 10 mins until the bread sounds hollow when tapped. Cool on a wire rack, then slice it into fingers to serve.

prosciutto san daniele e fichi
fresh figs with prosciutto

Figs wrapped in prosciutto is one of those classic, ultra-simple Italian combinations that relies totally on the quality and flavour of the ingredients. Figs are in season in early autumn, having ripened over the summer. Keep them in the fruit bowl, not the fridge, to enjoy the flavour at its best.

Prep time: 10 mins

SERVES 4

INGREDIENTS
8 slices Prosciutto San Daniele
8 fresh figs

Take the prosciutto out of the fridge 30 mins before serving – the ham should be at room temperature to bring out its full flavour.

Slice the figs in half and serve either with the ham, or wrap half a slice of ham around each fig half. It's as simple as that.

'Summer holidays in Portugal at Maurie and Suzy's farmhouse. Fresh figs from the tree!'

crostini con patè di olive nere
black olive tapenade

You need good-quality olives for this really simple dip, then just add whatever flavouring ingredients take your fancy.

Prep time: 10 mins

SERVES 6

INGREDIENTS
around 170g stoned black olives
½ garlic clove, peeled and crushed
1–2 tbsp olive oil
salt and freshly ground black pepper
1 tsp balsamic vinegar
leaves picked from 2–3 sprigs of thyme

Put the black olives and garlic in a food processor or mini blender with the oil, and whiz to a coarse-textured purée. Spoon into a bowl, season well and stir in the vinegar and thyme. Serve with focaccia or on crostini or bruschetta.

'What I love about Italian food is its simplicity'

funghi ripieni
stuffed mushrooms

Whoever said life's too short to stuff a mushroom didn't think about the man-sized, flat field or portobello ones, which are perfect for filling with ingredients. I like to get a taste of herbs from this dish – it marries well with the earthy flavour of the mushrooms.

Prep time: 10 mins
Cooking time: 20–30 mins

SERVES 4

INGREDIENTS

8 field or portobello mushrooms
125g ricotta cheese
3 spring onions, finely chopped
a couple of sage leaves, finely chopped
salt and freshly ground black pepper
25g Parmesan cheese, freshly grated
2 tsp olive oil, to drizzle

Preheat the oven to 200°C/180°C fan oven/gas mark 6.

Remove the stalk from each mushroom and place flat-side up into a roasting tin. You don't need the stalks for this recipe, but you can save them to use in soups, if you like.

Beat together the ricotta, spring onions and sage, and season well. Stir in half the grated cheese.

Divide the mixture equally among the mushrooms, sprinkle with the remaining cheese and drizzle with a little oil. Cook in the oven for 20–30 mins. Serve with ciabatta bread.

peperonata
mixed pepper medley

This is one of those wonderful recipes so typical of Italian cooking: a sweet vegetable stew that's rich with the natural juices of the peppers. It transforms a handful of ingredients into a lot more than the sum of their parts. Vincenzo, my father, passed this recipe down to me; his mother used to add a chopped potato to the pot, which makes it into a thicker, heartier dish. It tastes even better the day after and will keep for up to five days in the fridge, so I cook double the quantity and use it as a standby. It works well as a starter, goes with any main course and it's really useful when you're trying to perform the miracle of the loaves and fishes, when you unexpectedly find you've got a crowd to feed.

Prep time: 30 mins
Cooking time: 1 hour

SERVES 8

INGREDIENTS
3 tbsp olive oil
1 large onion, peeled and sliced
2 each red, orange and yellow peppers,
　finely sliced
salt and freshly ground black pepper
300g tomatoes, deseeded and chopped

Heat the oil in a pan and add the onion. Cook gently for around 15 mins, until softened. Add the peppers, season well, and cover. Continue to cook slowly over a low heat for 40 mins – there'll be enough liquid in the peppers to make a delicious natural stock.

Add the tomatoes and cook for a further 5 mins.

sacla' tip
For a real zing, add 2 tbsp Dallaglio by Sacla' Diavola sauce.

bruschetta di Vincenzo
Vincenzo's bruschetta

Bruschetta (pronounced with a 'k' rather than with a 'sh') can be topped with whatever takes your fancy. I like to keep it simple and put each topping in its own bowl so that people can help themselves to whatever they like.

Prep time: 15 mins
Cooking time: 5 mins

SERVES 4

INGREDIENTS

6 garlic cloves, peeled
100ml olive oil
ripe tomatoes
extra virgin olive oil
basil leaves
mozzarella, sliced
rocket
Parma ham
8 slices Italian bread (campagnola)

Make the garlic oil by slicing the garlic and putting it in a small pan with the olive oil. Heat gently for a few minutes over a very low heat, making sure the garlic doesn't turn golden, otherwise the flavour will be too strong and bitter. Set aside to cool.

Chop the tomatoes, put them in a bowl and drizzle with the extra virgin olive oil. Tear a few basil leaves and stir in. Put the remaining ingredients in separate bowls.

Lightly toast the bread and brush each slice with the garlic oil. Put on a plate with all the bowls filled with the other ingredients and let everyone make their own. Enjoy!

sacla' tip

Use Dallaglio by Sacla' Slow-Baked Tomatoes – either the Marinated With Garlic or the Marinated With Chilli. Also, try spreading a little Sacla' Classic Basil Pesto onto bruschetta before layering on the other ingredients.

carpaccio di manzo con rucola e grana
carpaccio of beef with rocket and parmesan

A good carpaccio relies on the quality of the beef, so buy from a good butcher who knows the farm where it was reared. It makes a stunning starter that can either be served on a platter for a big group of people, or on individual plates for a more intimate gathering.

Prep time: 10 mins, plus freezing time of 1 hour, plus 30 mins to reach room temperature

SERVES 4–6

INGREDIENTS
200g beef fillet
100g rocket
chunk of Parmesan cheese
extra virgin olive oil or, if you want to splash out, truffle oil
salt and freshly ground black pepper

Wrap the beef in clingfilm and freeze for about 1 hour.

Remove from the freezer and unwrap the clingfilm. Use a sharp meat knife to slice the beef into very thin rounds. Lay the slices on a plate and set aside for 30 mins to allow them to reach room temperature.

Garnish with the rocket and use a vegetable peeler to shave over enough Parmesan to generously feed four people. Drizzle with whichever oil you prefer and season.

grigliata di verdure
medley of grilled vegetables

This is inspired by a dish we love at Riva in Barnes, south London, our favourite restaurant that doubles as the Dallaglio family canteen. Use whatever vegetables you have to hand, but make sure you griddle them well so that they're properly cooked through. The mint adds a refreshing element and, if you like a kick of heat, use a red chilli instead of a green one.

Prep time: 10 mins
Cooking time: 40 mins

SERVES 4

INGREDIENTS
1 red pepper
1 yellow pepper
2 courgettes
1 aubergine
4 large flat portobello mushrooms
a little olive oil, for brushing
3–4 tbsp extra virgin olive oil
1 mild green chilli, chopped
salt and freshly ground black pepper
a few mint leaves, torn

Start by preparing the vegetables. Halve the peppers and remove the core, seeds and any white pith. Halve again.

Slice the courgettes lengthways. Slice the aubergine lengthways into three or four slices. Trim the stalks of the mushroom and brush off any soil.

Brush all the vegetables with oil and heat a griddle pan until hot. Griddle the vegetables in batches until tender enough to eat.

Transfer to a platter. Put the extra virgin olive oil in a bowl with the chilli and season well. Drizzle over the veg and garnish with the mint.

insalata di arance e finocchio
fennel and orange salad

For a salad to taste its best, take the ingredients out of the fridge a while before serving – they taste better at room temperature. A good dressing makes a salad, so make sure all the ingredients get coated, not just the ones nearest the top. Alice and the girls usually take care of this bit while Enzo and I do 'man's work'.

Prep time: 15 mins

SERVES 4

INGREDIENTS

4 tbsp extra virgin olive oil
1 tbsp white wine vinegar
salt and freshly ground black pepper
1 orange
1 small bulb of fennel
1 small head of radicchio or chicory
8 stoned black olives, halved
small handful of parsley

Put the oil and vinegar in a bowl and season well. Add 1 tsp cold water and whisk briefly.

Use a sharp, serrated knife to cut the top and bottom off the orange, then work around the orange, slicing away the skin and pith. Cut in between each piece of orange skin to extract the segments, and put them in a bowl with their juice.

Finely slice the fennel – use a mandolin if you've got one, but watch you don't slice your fingertips as you get close to the end of the vegetable. Add to the bowl. Separate the leaves of radicchio or chicory and add to the bowl, along with the black olives. Roughly chop the parsley and mix it in. Toss all the ingredients together and serve.

melanzane con pesto e mozzarella
aubergine with pesto and mozzarella

These are great as a lunchtime snack, but they're also smart enough to be part of an antipasto starter. You often hear people say that it's not necessary to salt aubergines, but I disagree: by drawing out the juices, the aubergines will absorb less fat when you fry them.

Prep time: 10 mins, plus salting time
Cooking time: 15 mins

SERVES 4

INGREDIENTS
1 aubergine
salt and freshly ground black pepper
2 tbsp olive oil
1–2 tbsp Sacla' Sun-dried Tomato Pesto
125g mozzarella, sliced

Slice the aubergine into eight rounds. Arrange the slices in a colander, sprinkling each layer with salt. Set aside for 20 mins to allow the salt to draw out the bitter juices. Rinse well.

Heat half the oil and fry the aubergine slices in two batches until golden on each side, adding the remaining oil to the second batch. Spread out on a baking sheet, spread a little pesto on top of each round and top with a slice of mozzarella. Grill until golden.

affettati misti con cipolline in agrodolce
sweet 'n' sour onions

Baby onions and shallots are a pain to peel – the papery skins stick to the bulb and it takes forever to remove the layers. I've found the quickest way is to tip them into a large bowl, cover with boiling water and leave them for about 5–10 minutes. When you drain the water, the skins come away easily. Job done.

Prep time: 15 mins
Cooking time: around 40 mins

SERVES 4

INGREDIENTS
2 tbsp olive oil
400g baby onions or shallots, peeled
2 garlic cloves, peeled and sliced
3 tbsp light muscovado sugar
200ml red wine vinegar
1 tsp finely chopped rosemary

Heat the oil in a small saucepan and cook the whole onions over a low heat until very soft, stirring every now and then for about 20 mins. Add a splash of water if the mixture looks dry.

Add the garlic and cook for 1–2 mins. Stir in the sugar, vinegar and rosemary, and bring to the boil. Cook, covered, for about 15 mins.

Remove the lid and continue to simmer until syrupy.

Serve with...
Affettati misti – a traditional plate of mixed, cured meats. If you have a good Italian deli nearby, ask them to give you a varied selection. It should be made up a bit like a cheese board, with a choice of different meats. I like to include a spicy salami and finocchiona, which is Tuscan salami made with fennel seeds.

impasto di piadina alla Dallaglio
Dallaglio's doughballs

I used to make these with my grandmother in Italy, then with my dad in London. Now it's my son Enzo's turn, and he loves making them. They're dead easy to make and ready for the oven as soon as the dough is shaped into balls. Plus, they cook really fast, which is a bonus as far as Enzo's concerned.

Prep time: 30 mins, plus rising and proving time
Cooking time: 10–12 mins

SERVES 4

INGREDIENTS

10g fresh yeast
300g strong plain flour
½ tsp salt
1 tsp olive oil
75g softened butter
1 garlic clove, peeled and crushed
1 tsp each chopped parsley and chives

sacla' tip

Warm half a jar of Dallaglio by Sacla' Napoletana sauce in a pan and serve alongside the doughballs.

Line a baking sheet with baking parchment. Put the yeast in a bowl and pour over 90ml lukewarm water.

Sift the flour into a separate bowl, stir in the salt and make a well in the centre. Pour in the yeast mixture, followed by another 90ml lukewarm water and the oil. Mix with a knife, then get your hands in there and bring the mixture together. Put the dough on a board and knead well. Resist adding any more flour – it should be soft and sticky. Set aside for 30 mins to rise.

Divide the dough into quarters, then divide each quarter into four or five pieces. Roll into small balls and place on the prepared baking sheet. Repeat with the remaining dough.

Preheat the oven to 200°C/180°C fan oven/gas mark 6. Bake for 10–12 mins until pale golden. The doughballs are ready when they sound hollow when tapped on the base.

In a bowl, beat together the butter, garlic and herbs. Season well. Serve with the doughballs.

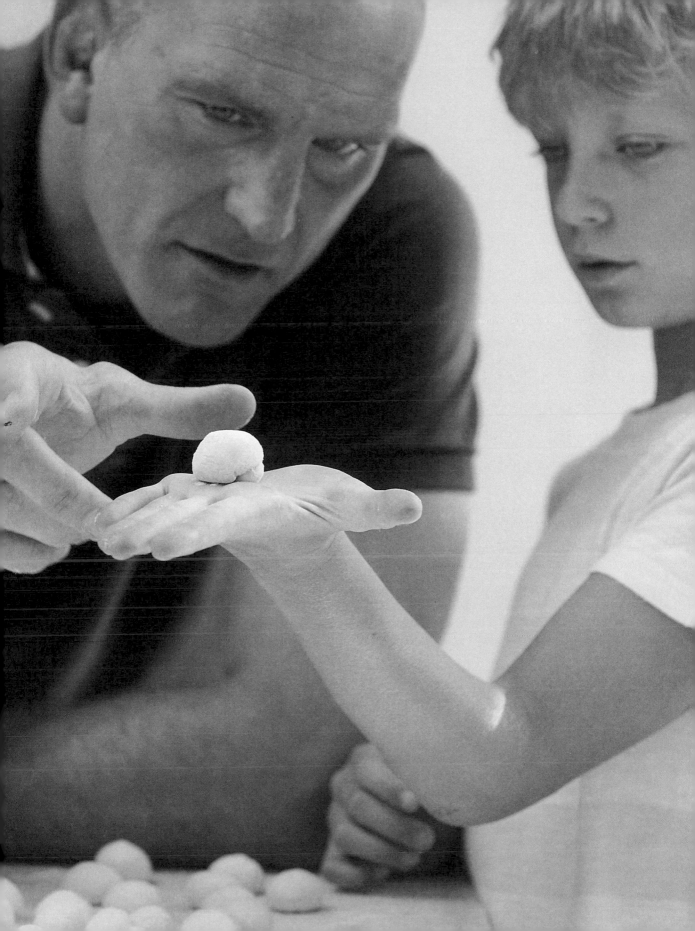

torta di pancetta e parmigiano
savoury pancetta muffins

This is a speedy recipe that you can make with the family. Serve it for brunch with eggs, beans and mushrooms, or as an afternoon snack. Add herbs if you like, but I've used my favourite ready-made pesto, which gives it a savoury punch.

Prep time: 15 mins
Cooking time: 25–30 mins

MAKES 6 MUFFINS

INGREDIENTS

100g pancetta
225g self-raising flour
50g Parmesan cheese, freshly grated
½ tsp salt
40g butter, melted and cooled
175g natural yoghurt
1 medium egg
2 tbsp Sacla' Organic Tomato Pesto

You'll need a six-hole muffin tin and six paper muffin cases; or a silicone muffin mould (which needs no lining).

Preheat the oven to 200°C/180°C fan oven/gas mark 6.

Put the pancetta in a frying pan and dry fry over a medium heat. Cook until golden and crispy. Tip onto a sheet of kitchen paper to drain any fat and leave to cool.

Put the flour, Parmesan and salt in a bowl. Add the cooled pancetta and toss together to mix.

In a separate bowl, beat together the cooled butter, yoghurt, egg and pesto. Make a well in the centre of the flour mixture and pour in the yoghurt mixture. Roughly mix together – there should still be some floury patches, but don't worry, it's meant to be like that.

Spoon into the muffin tin, piling the mixture high in each hole. Bake for 25–30 mins or until a skewer pushed into the middle comes out clean.

Remove from the tin and cool on a wire rack until just warm, then dive in.

vova alla fiorentina
eggs florentine

You'll find lots of recipes for eggs Florentine, but no one does it better than the Italians, who stick to the simplest form. There isn't any hollandaise or béchamel sauce; it's just spinach sautéed in butter, topped with an egg and baked in the oven. If you want to give the spinach a flavour boost, this is the time to use up any leftover sauces.

Prep time: 10 mins
Cooking time: 20 mins

SERVES 4

INGREDIENTS
500g spinach
15g butter
salt and freshly ground black pepper
4 medium eggs

Preheat the oven to 200°C/180°C fan oven/gas mark 6.

Wash the spinach well and shake off the excess water. Melt the butter in a pan and add the spinach. Season well, cover with a lid and cook for a few minutes until just wilted – you may need to toss it halfway through.

Divide the spinach among four shallow ovenproof dishes. Make a little well in the centre and crack an egg into each. Season, then bake in the oven for 15–17 mins until the egg is cooked but the yolk is still runny.

sacla' tip
Add a little Dallagio by Sacla' Napoletana sauce to the spinach.

'My dad Vincenzo, aged 8, with his two sisters, Giuseppina and Ernestina, at his First Holy Communion in 1941'

caponata siciliana
sicilian aubergine stew

Italians love vegetable stews and this one, with its rich aubergines, is a favourite among meat-lovers. It's an unusual dish, because it uses vinegar to give it sharpness, which is then balanced with sugar. Again, it improves with a day in the fridge to allow all the flavours to come together.

Prep time: 10 mins
Cooking time: 30 mins

SERVES 4

INGREDIENTS

2 large aubergines, chopped into chunks
2 tbsp olive oil
1 onion, peeled and chopped
2 sticks of celery, chopped
400g can chopped tomatoes
1 tsp caster sugar
2–3 tbsp red wine vinegar
50g pitted black olives

Put the chopped aubergine in a colander and sprinkle with salt. Set aside for 1 hour to extract the bitter juices. Rinse well.

Heat the oil in a large pan. Fry the onion on a low heat until softened, for about 10–15 mins. Add the celery and aubergine and cook for a further 5 mins.

Tip in the tomatoes and stir everything together. Add the sugar, vinegar and olives, cover with a lid and simmer for about 15 mins until reduced and sauce-like in texture.

frittelle di zucchine
courgette fritters

This recipe is very simple to make and tastes out of this world. You only need one courgette to make enough fritters for four people, so it takes hardly any time to prepare. Make sure you season the mixture, though, as courgettes can be bland. Sometimes I add a bit of lemon zest or a grating of nutmeg, which complements courgette well.

Prep time: 15 mins
Cooking time: 15 mins

SERVES 4

INGREDIENTS
1 medium egg
25g plain flour
salt and freshly ground black pepper
30g pecorino cheese, freshly grated
1 large courgette, grated
a couple of sage leaves, finely chopped
2 tsp olive oil

Beat together the egg and flour and season well. If you have time, set the mixture aside for 30 mins to allow the flour to be absorbed into the egg. Fold in the pecorino, grated courgette and sage.

Heat the oil in a frying pan and drop three or four tablespoonfuls of the mixture into it. Fry for a few minutes over a medium heat until golden, then turn over and cook on the other side. Repeat with the remaining mixture and serve immediately.

insalata di tonno e fagioli
tuna and bean salad

Italians are very fussy about the quality of their ingredients, and it particularly shows in their salads. For this one, you need to buy really good tuna — preserved in extra virgin olive oil — to get the best flavour.

Prep time: 15 mins

SERVES 4

INGREDIENTS

½ red onion, peeled and finely chopped
1 tbsp red wine vinegar
115g can tuna preserved in olive oil, drained
400g can cannellini beans, drained
1 tbsp capers
2 tbsp freshly chopped parsley
salt and freshly ground black pepper
4 Dallaglio by Sacla' Slow-Baked Tomatoes Marinated With Garlic, sliced
50g rocket
2 tbsp extra virgin olive oil

Put the onion in a little bowl with a pinch of salt and the vinegar. Toss well and set aside to marinate.

Put the drained tuna in a large salad bowl. Add the beans, capers and parsley and toss well. Season to taste.

Stir in the sliced tomatoes and rocket. Add the extra virgin olive oil to the red onion mixture and mix well. Pour over the salad, toss and serve.

prosciutto con finocchio al forno
baked fennel with parma ham

Poaching the fennel first in a little vegetable stock softens the wonderful aniseed flavour. Then it gets star treatment with a bit of cream, ricotta and Parma ham. This dish is pretty versatile: I serve it as a hot starter if we have friends round, and it's easily adjusted to suit vegetarians – just leave out the ham and scatter over freshly grated Parmesan instead. Make sure you've got plenty of crusty bread to go round.

Prep time: 10 mins
Cooking time: 20 mins

SERVES 4

INGREDIENTS
2 large fennel bulbs
200ml hot vegetable stock
50ml double cream
50g ricotta cheese
salt and freshly ground black pepper
4 slices Parma ham

Preheat the oven to 200°C/180°C fan oven/gas mark 6.

Cut each fennel bulb lengthways into four thick slices. Cut off the green fronds and reserve. Put the bulbs in a pan with the hot stock, cover and bring to the boil, then simmer for 5 mins until tender.

Lift out and transfer to an ovenproof dish. Stir the cream and ricotta into the stock in the pan and season well, then pour it over the fennel and place the Parma ham slices on top. Cook in the oven for 15 mins, by which time the sauce will be bubbling and the Parma ham crisp. Chop the reserved fronds and scatter on top.

piatti rapidi durante la settimana
quick weekday suppers

Organising the family and keeping on top of the hundred and one fixtures that dominate our household sometimes feels like herding cats. But we never stint on good, nutritious, weeknight food.

polpette alla diavola
meatballs with diavola sauce

This is a great basic way of making meatballs. If you prefer, you can use the mince mixture to make four hearty burgers and serve them in a bun with a dollop of the sauce.

Prep time: 15 mins
Cooking time: 15 mins

SERVES 4

INGREDIENTS
500g lean beef mince
1 tbsp freshly chopped parsley
1 tbsp freshly chopped basil
4 spring onions, chopped
zest of 1 lemon
100g breadcrumbs
pinch of ground cinnamon
salt and freshly ground black pepper
a little olive oil
300g jar Dallaglio by Sacla'
    Diavola sauce
400g penne pasta
freshly grated Parmesan cheese

Bring a large pan of salted water to the boil.

Put the mince in a bowl with the herbs, spring onions, lemon zest, breadcrumbs and cinnamon. Mix it all together and season well.

Take walnut-sized pieces of the mince and roll into balls. Heat a little olive oil in a pan and fry the meatballs lightly until golden.

Heat the sauce in a pan and add the meatballs.

Meanwhile, cook the penne in the boiling water until al dente. Add a ladleful of pasta water to the sauce and meatballs – this will loosen the mixture and help bring all the flavours together.

Drain the pasta well. Return it to the pan and add the meatballs and sauce. Toss everything together. Divide among four bowls, sprinkle with Parmesan and serve immediately.

linguine con zucchine
linguine with courgettes

This is a classic from southern Italy and is incredibly quick to make. It's as simple as flavouring the oil with garlic first, then frying the slices of courgette in the oil.

Prep time: 10 mins
Cooking time: 20 mins

SERVES 4

INGREDIENTS

2 tbsp olive oil
2 garlic cloves, peeled and thinly sliced
4 small courgettes, thinly sliced
400g linguine
freshly grated Parmesan cheese
salt and freshly ground black pepper

Bring a large pan of salted water to the boil.

Heat 1 tbsp of the oil in a large pan and gently cook the garlic until soft. Lift out and set aside on a plate.

Add half the courgettes to the pan, spreading them out in an even layer, and fry until golden on each side, seasoning with salt as you go. Lift out onto the plate with the garlic. Pour the remaining tbsp oil into the pan and cook the rest of the courgettes.

Meanwhile, cook the linguine until al dente. Drain the pasta, leaving a little water clinging to the strands. Return to the pan and add the fried courgettes and garlic. Toss all the ingredients together and divide among four bowls.

Sprinkle with Parmesan and serve immediately with a little freshly ground pepper, if you like.

spaghettini all'amatriciana
spaghettini with tomato and bacon sauce

This differs from arrabbiata in that it includes pancetta. Once you've fried the pancetta, make sure you drain the fat away, otherwise the sauce could be a bit greasy. I've used spaghettini here because, for me, it feels a bit lighter.

Prep time: 15 mins
Cooking time: 15 mins

SERVES 4

INGREDIENTS

70g pancetta, cut into small cubes
2 tsp olive oil
1 small garlic clove, peeled and crushed
pinch of chilli flakes
50ml dry white wine
400g can chopped plum tomatoes
salt and freshly ground black pepper
400g spaghettini
a few chopped basil leaves
freshly grated pecorino cheese

Bring a large pan of salted water to the boil.

Heat a frying pan and dry fry the pancetta – you won't need oil, as there's enough fat from the meat. When it's cooked, drain off the fat and place on kitchen paper.

Heat the oil in a pan and gently fry the garlic and chilli flakes until you can just smell the aroma of the garlic cooking in the pan. Add the wine and cook until it has reduced by about half. Tip in the pancetta and tomatoes and season well. Bring to the boil and cook the sauce quickly, adding a ladleful of water to the sauce.

Meanwhile, cook the spaghettini until al dente. Drain the pasta, leaving a little water clinging to the strands. Return to the pan, add half the sauce and stir well, then divide among four plates and top with the remaining sauce and pecorino.

orecchiette con broccoletti e alici
pasta with broccoli, chilli and anchovies

Packed with vegetables, this is a healthy and well-balanced dish. The anchovies give it a tangy saltiness, while the chilli lends a cheeky kick. *Orecchiette* means 'little ears', a perfect shape for trapping and holding the ingredients.

Prep time: 5 mins
Cooking time: 15 mins

SERVES 4

INGREDIENTS

1 small tin anchovies in oil, chopped
1 garlic clove, peeled and sliced
pinch of chilli flakes
½ red pepper, deseeded and chopped
2 plum tomatoes, chopped
400g dried orecchiette pasta
1 head of broccoli
½ lemon, cut into 4 wedges, to serve

sacla' tip
Save time and use a 300g jar of Dallaglio by Sacla' Diavola sauce instead of tomatoes and pepper.

Heat about 1 tbsp oil from the anchovy tin (discard the rest) in a pan and add the garlic and chilli flakes. Cook for 1 min. Add the red pepper and tomatoes. Heat gently, then add the anchovies and allow them to melt into the sauce.

Bring a large pan of salted water to the boil and cook the orecchiette until al dente. Cut the broccoli into florets and peel the stem, discarding the tough skin. Chop the stem into bite-sized chunks.

About 4 mins before the end of the pasta cooking time, add a ladleful of water to the pepper, tomato and anchovy sauce, then drop the broccoli florets into the pan with the pasta. Cook until the pasta is al dente.

Drain the pasta and broccoli well. Return to the pan and pour in the sauce. Toss together, then divide among four bowls and serve with a wedge of lemon to squeeze over.

gnocchi ripieni di ricotta e spinaci
ricotta and spinach dumplings

If you're thinking that all this spinach makes these dumplings a bit dull and worthy, you'd be wrong. Mixed together with ricotta and lemon, they are transformed into bite-sized angel food. Serve with a drizzle of melted butter, Parmesan and plenty of freshly ground black pepper.

Prep time: 20 mins
Cooking time: 15 mins

SERVES 4

INGREDIENTS
500g spinach
250g ricotta cheese
zest of 1 lemon
1 medium egg, lightly beaten
1 tsp salt
50g plain flour, plus extra for dusting
melted butter and freshly grated Parmesan
   cheese, to serve

Sacla' tip
You can also bake this dish. Put the dumplings in an overproof dish, spoon over Dallaglio by Sacla' Tricolore sauce, top with 2–3 tbsp breadcrumbs and bake in a hot oven until bubbling and golden.

Lightly cook the spinach, drain it well and squeeze as much of the water out as possible. Allow to cool.

Roughly chop the spinach and put it in a bowl with the ricotta, lemon zest, egg and salt. Mix everything together, adding the flour, to bring all the ingredients together.

Take walnut-sized pieces of the mixture and roll into balls, using a little flour.

Bring a large pan of salted water to the boil and add the dumplings in batches. When you first drop them in they'll sink to the bottom, but when they're cooked they'll rise to the top and float there – lift them out with a slotted spoon and set aside until you've cooked all of them. Divide among four plates, drizzle with melted butter and top with grated Parmesan.

tagliatelle con gorgonzola e noci
gorgonzola and walnut tagliatelle

This is as quick as it gets to rustle up a cooked supper – it's done while the pasta's cooking. The strong, punchy flavour comes from the Italian blue-veined cheese, Gorgonzola, while crunchy nuts give it a bit of attitude. Serve it with plenty of freshly ground black pepper.

Prep and cooking time: 10 mins

SERVES 4

INGREDIENTS

400g tagliatelle
200g Gorgonzola cheese
25g butter
25g walnuts, roughly chopped
2 tbsp freshly chopped parsley
salt and freshly ground black pepper

Bring a large pan of salted water to the boil and cook the tagliatelle until al dente, following the timings on the pack – it's usually around 10 mins.

Chop the cheese and put it in a small pan. Heat gently until half melted – it will continue to melt once you toss it into the pasta.

Drain the pasta, leaving a little water clinging to the pasta. Return it to the pan and add the butter. Toss well, stir in the cheese, nuts and parsley and season well. Divide among four bowls and serve immediately.

'It's taken a while to get the kids to love Gorgonzola as much as Alice and I do...'

stufato di verdure alla ligure
italian-style ratatouille

This tastes even better the day after. You need a wide pan so that the vegetables have a chance to cook first in the oil and don't lie on top of one another and sweat. Cooking the veg in stages may look like more trouble than it's worth, but it allows you to sauté each batch, which maximises the flavour in the finished dish. It's fantastic with a roast.

Prep time: 20 mins, plus salting time
Cooking time: around 45 mins

SERVES 4

INGREDIENTS

1 aubergine, chopped into chunks
2–3 tbsp olive oil
1 onion, peeled and sliced
1 garlic clove, peeled and sliced
1 red pepper, deseeded and chopped
1 large courgette, chopped
200g can chopped tomatoes
1 tbsp tomato purée
200ml hot vegetable stock
2 bay leaves
salt and freshly ground black pepper
1 tsp balsamic vinegar
handful of basil leaves

Put the chopped aubergine in a colander and sprinkle with salt. Set aside for 30 mins to extract the bitter juices. Rinse well.

Heat half the oil in a wide saucepan and sauté the onion for 10 mins over a medium heat until softened. Add the garlic and cook for 1 min. Add the aubergine to the pan with the remaining oil. Cook for a further 10 mins until golden all over.

Add the pepper and courgette and cook for 5 mins, then add the tomatoes, tomato purée, hot stock and bay leaves. Season well. Cover and bring to the boil, then turn the heat down to a simmer and cook for 15–20 mins. Whip the bay leaves out and discard. Add the vinegar to the pan, then roughly tear the basil leaves, stir in and serve.

gnocchi alla diavola
gnocchi and tomato bake

This is comfort food at its best. Homemade gnocchi require just two ingredients – potatoes and flour – so easy that my kids can make them, and much lighter than the ones you buy in the supermarket. Season the dough well, otherwise the gnocchi will taste bland. I like mine in a spicy sauce, so once they're ready, I spoon over my Diavola sauce and sprinkle them with Parmesan.

Prep time: 35 mins, plus 1 hour chilling
Cooking time: 35 mins

SERVES 4

INGREDIENTS
650g floury potatoes, such as King Edwards, peeled
½ tsp salt
250g plain flour, plus extra to dust
300g jar Dallaglio by Sacla' Diavola sauce
freshly ground black pepper
freshly grated Parmesan cheese

Chop the potatoes into small chunks and steam them until tender. Lift the steamer, place the potato chunks in a bowl and set aside to dry for a few minutes.

Press the potatoes through a potato ricer into a bowl, or mash very thoroughly. Season with the salt and add the flour gradually, stirring it in with a wooden spoon to make a smooth, firm dough. This is like making bread – you might not need to add all the flour, so add it a little at a time. Put the dough on a board and roll it in your hands to make a sausage shape, then wrap it in clingfilm and chill for 1 hour.

Bring a large pan of salted water to the boil. Pour the Diavola sauce into a separate pan and heat gently. Preheat the oven to 200°C/180°C fan oven/gas mark 6.

Unwrap the dough and place it on a board. Dust lightly with a little flour to stop it sticking, then cut off a quarter. Roll this into a sausage shape a little thicker than your thumb, then cut off pieces the length of a finger. Repeat with the rest of the dough until you have a board full of little gnocchi.

Drop about 10 gnocchi into the pan of boiling water in one go and cook in batches. They're ready when they float to the top. Lift out with a slotted spoon and place in an ovenproof dish. Cover each batch with a spoonful of sauce and a little grated Parmesan, seasoning as you go. Continue until all the gnocchi are cooked and all the sauce is used. Bake in the preheated oven for about 10 mins until hot.

pasta alla ligure
italian riviera-style pasta

The traditional pasta to use for this dish is trofie. If you can't get hold of it, use shell-shaped conchiglie or linguine, which catch the pesto sauce well.

Prep time: 5 mins
Cooking time: 10 mins

SERVES 4

INGREDIENTS

400g trofie, conchiglie or linguine
2 medium salad or waxy potatoes, peeled and chopped
150g green beans, trimmed and halved
120g Sacla' Classic Basil Pesto
salt and freshly ground black pepper
freshly grated Parmesan cheese

Bring a large pan of salted water to the boil and cook the pasta according to the timings on the pack.

After half the cooking time, add the potatoes and green beans to the pan, cover and bring to the boil again. Remove the lid and continue to cook for the allotted time or until the pasta is al dente. Drain, leaving a little of the cooking water clinging to the pasta. Add the pesto, season and toss all the ingredients together.

Divide among four bowls and grate over a little Parmesan before serving.

risotto primavera
risotto with peas and asparagus

Italian food is a celebration of the seasons, which is why this recipe is so typical: it brings together all the late spring vegetables just as they're starting to appear in the shops and on market stalls.

Prep time: 15 mins
Cooking time: 30 mins

SERVES 4

INGREDIENTS

1 tbsp olive oil, plus extra for frying
25g butter
1 large onion, peeled and finely chopped
1.4 litres hot chicken stock
400g Arborio risotto rice
100ml dry white wine
salt
150g fresh peas
325g fresh asparagus spears,
    roughly chopped
freshly grated Parmesan cheese

Heat the oil and butter in a pan and cook the onion over a low heat until softened – this will take around 15–20 mins.

Pour the hot stock into a pan and bring to a gentle simmer.

Stir the rice into the onion and cook for 1 min. Pour in the white wine and allow it to reduce, then with the stock just simmering, add it ladleful by ladleful, stirring it into the rice to allow it to be absorbed. Continue to cook, adding the stock slowly, until it has all been absorbed by the rice, seasoning it along the way.

While the rice is cooking, put a little water in a pan and steam the peas. Drain and set aside. In a separate pan, gently fry the asparagus in a little oil until tender.

When the rice is cooked, stir in the peas and asparagus, then divide among four bowls and top each with a little freshly grated Parmesan.

sacla' tip
Stir two finely chopped Sacla' Artichoke Antipasti into the risotto at the end.

rigatoni alla puttanesca
tart's pasta

There are as many recipes for this particular pasta sauce as there are regions in Italy. As the name suggests, it's big-hearted, rough and ready, so the flavours are accordingly bold and punchy.

Prep time: 10 mins
Cooking time: 15 mins

SERVES 4

INGREDIENTS

1 tbsp olive oil
2 garlic cloves, peeled and roughly
   chopped
4 anchovies in olive oil
pinch of chilli flakes
10 black olives, chopped
1 tbsp capers
400g can chopped tomatoes
salt and freshly ground black pepper
400g rigatoni
2 tbsp freshly chopped parsley

Heat the oil in a shallow pan and add the garlic, anchovies and chilli flakes. Heat gently to allow the anchovies to melt into the oil and the garlic to gently release its flavour.

Stir in the black olives, capers and chopped tomatoes. Season well, bring to the boil and simmer for 15 mins.

Bring a large pan of salted water to the boil. Cook the rigatoni until al dente. Add a ladleful of pasta water to the pan to loosen the sauce. Drain the pasta well, return to the pan and add a little olive oil. Add the sauce and the parsley, and adjust the seasoning if necessary. Toss everything together, then divide among four bowls and serve.

pasta e ceci
chickpea and pasta stew

Here's the fast version of this very old peasant dish. I've fiddled with the recipe for reasons of 'health by stealth', to make sure I get a wide enough range of vegetables into the kids – that's why I use peppers, too.

Prep time: 15 mins
Cooking time: 25 mins

SERVES 4

INGREDIENTS
2 tbsp olive oil
1 onion, peeled and chopped
1 large carrot, peeled and chopped
1 celery stick, chopped
½ garlic clove, peeled and crushed
1 yellow pepper, deseeded and chopped
pinch of chilli flakes
1 sprig of rosemary
400g can chickpeas, drained
200g can chopped tomatoes
2 tsp tomato purée
500ml hot vegetable stock
1 bay leaf
salt and freshly ground black pepper
100g small-shaped pasta for soups
freshly grated Parmesan cheese and
    extra virgin olive oil, to serve

Heat the oil in a pan and add the onion, carrot and celery. Cook for about 10–15 mins until the vegetables have softened. Add the garlic, pepper, chilli flakes and rosemary, and stir in and cook for a further 5 mins.

Add the chickpeas, tomatoes, tomato purée, hot stock and bay leaf. Season well. Cover, bring to the boil, then simmer for 10 mins. Add the pasta to the pan and stir. Cover again and cook the pasta until al dente over a low heat for the time stated on the pack.

Divide among four bowls and serve with the grated Parmesan and a generous drizzle of oil.

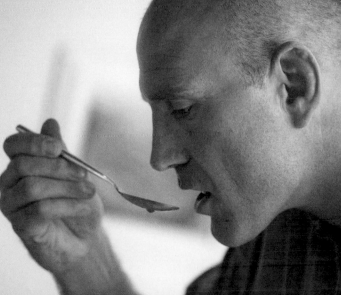

ragù alla bolognese
spaghettini bolognese

The traditional pasta for this sauce is tagliatelle, but my father uses spaghettini, a thinner version of spaghetti. It's lighter than egg pasta and the sauce coats it beautifully. We make double the amount of sauce, with the intention of freezing some, but it has yet to make it as far as the freezer.

Prep time: 30 mins
Cooking time: 45 mins

SERVES 4

INGREDIENTS

2 tbsp vegetable oil or olive oil
1 large onion, peeled and finely chopped
2 sticks of celery, finely chopped
2 medium carrots, peeled and finely chopped
500g beef mince
100g chopped rindless pancetta
1 garlic clove, peeled and chopped
100ml red wine
300ml passata
400g can chopped tomatoes
1 tsp tomato purée
1 beef stock cube
bouquet garni (a bay leaf, a few parsley stalks, a few sprigs of thyme)
dash of Worcestershire sauce
pinch of demerara sugar
salt and freshly ground black pepper
400g spaghettini
basil leaves
freshly grated Parmesan cheese

sacla' tip

Vincenzo's famous bolognese was the inspiration behind the delicious Dallaglio by Sacla' Bolognese sauce. If time is tight, just brown the mince in a pan, then add the jar of sauce and simmer for 10 mins.

Heat 1 tbsp of the oil in a large saucepan and fry the onion, celery and carrots – this base mixture is what the Italians call the *soffrito*. Cook gently until softened.

In a separate pan, heat the remaining tbsp oil and cook the mince, turning it every now and then until browned and golden.

In another pan, dry fry the pancetta – you won't need any oil as pancetta has enough fat in it already.

When the *soffrito* has softened, stir in the garlic and cook for 1 min.

Drain the mince through a sieve that's resting over a bowl. Add it to the *soffrito*. Do the same with the pancetta and add it to the pan. Discard the fat from both.

Add 50ml wine to each pan in which the mince and pancetta have been cooking to deglaze the pans, then add the juices to the pan with the mince mixture.

Add the passata, the chopped tomatoes, the tomato purée and the beef stock cube with the bouquet garni and 200ml water to the mince. Stir together with the Worcestershire sauce and the sugar. Season well and bring to a gentle simmer, cooking, uncovered, for 30 mins.

Bring a large pan of salted water to the boil. Add the spaghettini and cook until al dente. Add a ladleful of pasta water to the ragù – this helps to loosen the mixture and bring all the ingredients together.

Drain the pasta and return it to the pan. Add the sauce and toss everything together with a few freshly chopped basil leaves. Divide among four bowls and serve immediately with a little grated Parmesan.

pizza Enzo
Enzo's pizza

Pizza-making is a boys' job in our house, so three generations of Dallaglio males (Enzo, Vicenzo and me) get stuck in together, generating a snowstorm of flour. This is Enzo's all-time favourite.

Prep time: 30 mins
Cooking time: 8–10 mins for each pizza

SERVES 4

INGREDIENTS

15g fresh yeast
around 200–220ml lukewarm water
450g strong plain flour, plus extra for dusting
1 tsp salt
200ml passata
200g salame piccante
2 balls of mozzarella, sliced
drizzle of olive oil
salt and freshly ground black pepper
a few fresh basil leaves

sacla' tip

Slice some Dallaglio by Sacla' Italian Slow-Baked Tomatoes Marinated With Garlic and scatter over the pizzas before baking.

Preheat the oven to 220°C/200°C fan oven/gas mark 7. Preheat a couple of baking sheets or use a pizza stone if you have one (remember, with one stone, you'll only be able to cook one pizza at a time). To make the dough, put the yeast in a small bowl and add a little of the water. Stir to dissolve the yeast.

Put the flour in a large bowl and stir in the salt. Make a well in the centre and add the yeast liquid and the remaining water. Stir with a knife to bring the ingredients together.

When the mixture starts to look like dough, gather it up from the bowl with your hands and knead it on a floured board for about 10–15 mins until soft, smooth and elastic.

Divide the dough into quarters and tear off four pieces of baking parchment, each roughly 40cm square. Lightly dust with flour. Roll out each piece of dough into a circle on the parchment. This makes it easier to slide them onto the preheated baking sheet, giving you a thin and crispy base.

Spoon over a little passata, then add a few slices of salami and mozzarella. Drizzle with oil, season and slide the paper onto the baking sheets or pizza stone. Bake for 8–10 mins until crisp and golden. Cook the remaining pizzas. Garnish with basil leaves.

nodini al burro e salvia
veal cutlets with butter and sage

I love veal cooked this way. The sage is cooked with the butter, oil and meat and adds real depth of flavour to the finished dish. Make sure you cook the veal thoroughly – there shouldn't be a hint of pink. Pork chops are always an option for this dish, however, if you prefer.

Prep time: 10 mins
Cooking time: 15–20 mins

SERVES 4

INGREDIENTS
4 veal cutlets
salt and freshly ground black pepper
a little vegetable oil
a knob of butter
a few sage leaves
mashed potato and wilted spinach,
   to serve

Season the veal cutlets.

Heat the oil and butter in a large non-stick frying pan. When the butter stops foaming, add the cutlets and cook over a low to medium heat until golden. Turn over and cook the other side.

When the meat is almost cooked, add the sage to the pan, allocating some to each cutlet, and cook for a little longer.

Lift each cutlet onto a plate, garnishing with a drizzle of the herby oil and butter mixture, then spoon on some mashed potato and spinach and serve immediately.

'Veal is very lean and fine-textured, so be careful not to let it dry out when you're cooking it'

spaghetti con aglio e scampi
spaghetti with prawns and garlic

If you can't get hold of raw prawns, use cooked ones, but add them right at the very end when the oil mixture is in the pan with the pasta to prevent them from overcooking and becoming tough.

Prep time: 5 mins
Cooking time: 15 mins

SERVES 4

INGREDIENTS

400g spaghetti
1 tbsp olive oil
1 fresh chilli, chopped
1 garlic clove, peeled and sliced
300g raw prawns
4 Dallaglio by Sacla' Italian Slow-Baked
   Tomatoes Marinated With Chilli,
   sliced
salt and freshly ground black pepper
2 tbsp freshly chopped parsley

Bring a large pan of salted water to the boil and cook the spaghetti until al dente.

Heat the oil in a pan – a frying pan is good for this recipe – and add the chilli and garlic. Cook gently for about 1 min. Add the prawns and cook for a few minutes until they start to turn pink. Add a splash of cooking water from the pasta at this stage to help them on their way. Stir in the tomatoes and season.

Drain the pasta, then return it to the pan with the prawn mixture and parsley. Toss well and divide among four bowls.

'Fish and liver are brilliant sources of protein, great for repairing wear and tear – I ate loads of it as a rugby player, but kids need to get enough, too'

fegato di vitello alla veneziana
calf's liver with onions

This is one of my father's favourite recipes. It's full of flavour and rich in iron, and needs nothing more than a spoonful of creamy mash and green beans. Ask the butcher to slice the calf's liver for you.

Prep time: 15 mins
Cooking time: 20 mins

SERVES 4

INGREDIENTS
1 tbsp olive oil
1 onion, peeled and finely sliced
15g butter
500g calf's liver, cut into strips
salt and freshly ground black pepper
1 tbsp freshly chopped parsley
mashed potato and steamed green beans,
    to serve

Heat the oil in a pan and fry the onion on a low heat for about 15 mins until softened. Tip onto a plate and set aside.

Add the butter to the pan and allow it to melt, then add the calf's liver and cook over a medium heat, tossing every now and then, until cooked.

Return the onions to the pan with the liver, season well, then add the parsley. Toss everything together and serve immediately with mashed potato and steamed green beans.

pesce al pesto
pesto-topped fish

This is as easy as falling off a log – and it's ready in 20 minutes. Serve it simply with a green salad and boiled new potatoes.

Prep time: 5 mins
Cooking time: around 15 mins

SERVES 4

INGREDIENTS
1½ tbsp olive oil
25g stoned green olives, roughly chopped
3 tbsp Sacla' Classic Basil Pesto
zest of ½ lemon
4 x 125g pieces haddock loin
1 slice bread, whizzed into breadcrumbs
Parmesan cheese
salt and freshly ground black pepper
½ lemon, cut into four wedges

Preheat the oven to 200°C/180°C fan oven/gas mark 6.

Put the oil, olives, pesto and lemon zest in a mini food processor and whiz to make a paste.

Put the fish pieces in an ovenproof dish and top each piece with the pesto mixture. Sprinkle the breadcrumbs evenly over the pesto, and then grate some Parmesan on top.

Season well, then cook in the oven for about 15 mins until the fish is opaque in the middle. Serve with a wedge of lemon to squeeze over.

panzanella
tomato and bread salad

This recipe is ridiculously simple. It's a traditional peasant dish that's perfect for using up a glut of over-ripe tomatoes and bread that's gone stale in the heat of summer. But wait till you taste it – it's bursting with flavour and makes a perfect light lunch in warm weather.

Prep time: 15 mins

SERVES 4

INGREDIENTS
600g ripe tomatoes
1 small red onion, peeled
1 tbsp red wine vinegar
salt and freshly ground black pepper
¼ stale country-style loaf
2–3 tbsp extra virgin olive oil
fresh basil leaves

Halve the tomatoes and use a spoon to scoop out the seeds into a sieve resting over a bowl to catch the juices. Chop the tomatoes roughly and tip into a salad bowl.

Slice the red onion and add to the tomatoes with the red wine vinegar. Season and toss well.

Cut the bread into bite-sized chunks and add to the tomatoes with the olive oil. Toss everything together and add the basil leaves. If you can, cover and set this aside at room temperature for 30 mins to 1 hour before eating. The flavours will mix together and be all the better for it.

cozze alla marinara
fisherman's mussels

This recipe calls for just five ingredients. Mussels have bags of flavour, so they need very little embellishment. My kids use an empty shell to pick the mussels out of the other shells. Serve with plenty of crusty bread to mop up the juices.

Prep time: 20 mins
Cooking time: 5 mins

SERVES 4

INGREDIENTS
1 kg mussels
1 tbsp olive oil
1 garlic clove, peeled and crushed
125ml dry white wine
2 tbsp freshly chopped parsley
crusty bread, to serve

Pick over the mussels and discard any that are broken or remain open when tapped. Rinse well.

Heat the oil in a large pan and gently cook the garlic until just golden. Add the mussels, cover the pan and leave on the hob over a medium heat for a few minutes to steam open.

Add the wine to the pan, cover and bring to the boil. Cook for 1–2 mins.

Sprinkle over the parsley and serve immediately with crusty bread.

'Vincenzo, aged 16, and friends, waiting tables in Valentino Park in Torino in the summer of 1950'

risotto alla milanese
risotto with saffron

This simple and traditional risotto is flavoured with saffron, the world's most expensive spice, and it's one of my all-time favourites.

Prep time: 10 mins
Cooking time: 25 mins

SERVES 4

INGREDIENTS

40g butter
1 tbsp olive oil
1 large onion, peeled and chopped
400g Arborio risotto rice
pinch of saffron
1.4 litres hot vegetable or chicken stock
125ml dry white wine
salt
freshly grated Parmesan cheese

Melt 25g of the butter in a pan over a low heat with the oil. Add the onion and sauté for about 15 mins until softened. Stir in the risotto rice and saffron, and toss around in the mixture for a couple of minutes to coat and heat up the rice.

Pour the hot stock into a pan and bring to a gentle simmer.

Add the white wine and allow it to be absorbed by the rice. Then add the hot stock, one ladleful at a time, allowing each ladleful to be absorbed before adding the next one, stirring constantly. Continue cooking the rice in this way until all the stock is used up and the rice is tender, with a firm bite.

Add the remaining butter, season well and stir in some Parmesan. Divide among four bowls and grate over more cheese if you want.

'Piedmont, where my father, Vincenzo, grew up, has abundant rice harvests — so he takes his risotto very seriously indeed'

frittata di cipolle e piselli
frittata with onions and peas

The omelette is another inventive way that the Italians use up leftovers.
Do as they do – raid the fridge and include anything you fancy (even leftover
pasta). Whisk the eggs well to get lots of air into them, which makes the
mixture light and fluffy.

Prep and cooking time: 20 mins

SERVES 4

INGREDIENTS

200g peas
2 tbsp olive oil
2 large sweet onions, peeled and sliced
6 large eggs
salt and freshly ground black pepper
2 tbsp freshly chopped parsley
salad and crusty bread, to serve

Steam the peas in a pan until just tender and then drain.

Heat the oil in a large non-stick pan and sweat the onions for
about 15 mins until soft and just starting to turn golden.

Beat the eggs in a bowl with a whisk and season well. Stir in the
parsley. Preheat the grill.

Pour the egg mixture into the pan with the onions, then sprinkle
with the peas. Use a wooden spoon to loosen the mixture as it
cooks and sticks to the bottom, and allow the uncooked egg to
run into the 'holes'. Cook until the egg is almost cooked, then
grill until golden. Serve with a salad and crusty bread.

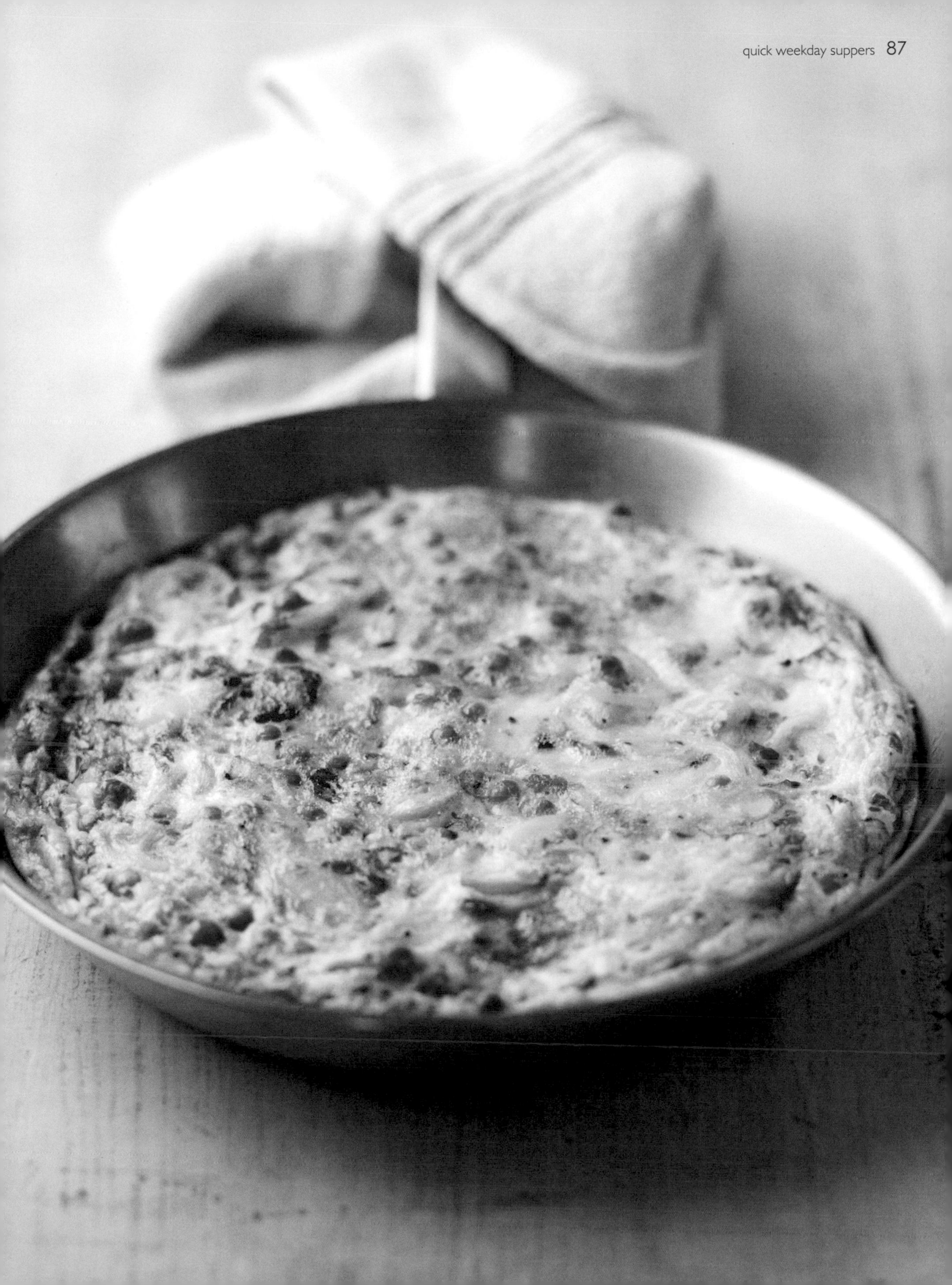

per gli amici di casa

weekend food for friends

3

These recipes are typical of what we cook at laid-back gatherings of family and friends. Nothing beats getting together around a table for catching up with what matters most – the people you care about.

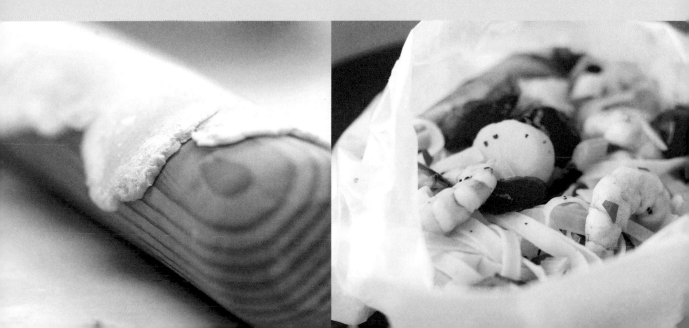

melanzane alla parmigiana
aubergine bake with parmesan

A sumptuous dish that I make when we have vegetarian friends over. The meat-eaters are invariably satisfied, too, as it's so rich. Serve with a green salad and some crusty bread.

Prep time: 25 mins, plus salting time
Cooking time: 40–50 mins

SERVES 4

INGREDIENTS

2 aubergines, sliced to the thickness
  of a £1 coin
3 tbsp olive oil
1 onion, peeled and finely chopped
1 carrot, peeled and finely chopped
1 celery stick, finely chopped
400g can chopped tomatoes
50g freshly grated Parmesan cheese
1–2 balls of mozzarella, thinly sliced
salt and freshly ground black pepper

Place the aubergine slices in a colander and salt each layer. Set aside for 20 mins to extract the bitter juices. Rinse well.

Heat 1 tbsp of the oil in a pan and fry the onion, carrot and celery until softened and just starting to turn golden. Add the chopped tomatoes, with a splash of water to rinse out the can, and bring to the boil. Simmer for 10 mins until it's the consistency of a sauce.

Preheat the oven to 200°C/180°C fan oven/gas mark 6. Meanwhile, fry the aubergines in a pan in the remaining oil until tender on each side.

Take a 1.2-litre ovenproof dish and spoon a little tomato sauce on the base. Layer up the aubergine, Parmesan, tomato sauce and mozzarella, finishing with a layer of mozzarella. Season as you go. Lastly, sprinkle with Parmesan.

Bake in the preheated oven for about 20–30 mins, until bubbling and golden.

sacla' tip

If you're pushed for time, use a 300g jar of Dallaglio by Sacla' Tricolore sauce instead of making the tomato sauce.

abbacchio alla romana
roman-style lamb chops in anchovy and rosemary sauce

This is a classic Roman dish. It's rich and gutsy, so no need for anything more than plain boiled potatoes to go with it, plus, maybe, spinach wilted in butter, or some green beans.

Prep time: 10 mins
Cooking time: 50 mins

SERVES 4

INGREDIENTS

2 tbsp plain flour
salt and freshly ground black pepper
8 lamb cutlets
1 tbsp sunflower oil
2 garlic cloves, peeled and sliced
600ml hot lamb or chicken stock
3 tbsp white wine vinegar
4 anchovies in oil, roughly chopped
2 sprigs of rosemary, roughly chopped

Preheat the oven to 200°C/180°C fan oven/gas mark 6.

Put the flour in a shallow bowl and season well. Dip each lamb cutlet in the seasoned flour to coat.

Heat the oil in a large frying pan. Fry the lamb in batches until golden on each side. Set aside. Add the garlic and remaining flour to the pan and cook for 1–2 mins.

Pour in the hot stock and the vinegar and stir continuously to mix in the flour. Add the anchovies and rosemary and return the cutlets to the pan. Cover and bring to the boil, then transfer to the oven and cook for 30 mins. The sauce will have thickened to a rich gravy and the lamb will be tender.

Try this wine with it...
Luigi d'Alessandro, Cortona Syrah (Tuscany)
Red

scaloppine di pollo alla milanese
milanese chicken breasts

Here's a recipe that my kids can't get enough of. It's basically chicken breasts flattened, then coated in breadcrumbs mixed with thyme and rosemary. You can be generous with the herbs, as that guarantees plenty of flavour. If you want to max the healthiness factor, bake in the oven at 200°C/180°C fan oven/ gas mark 6 for 20 minutes instead of frying. It will come out pale gold and equally delicious. Serve it up with a green salad.

Prep time: 15 mins
Cooking time: 20 mins

SERVES 4

INGREDIENTS

4 skinless chicken breasts
3 tbsp plain flour
2 large eggs, beaten
2 slices white bread, whizzed into
   breadcrumbs
4 sprigs of thyme, freshly chopped
2 sprigs of rosemary, freshly chopped
salt and freshly ground black pepper
a little sunflower oil

Line a chopping board with clingfilm, place two of the chicken breasts on it, then cover with another sheet of clingfilm. Bash them with a rolling pin until they're flattened – ideally they should be about 0.5cm thick. Repeat with the other two breasts.

Put the flour in a shallow bowl, the beaten eggs in another, and the breadcrumbs in yet another. Add the herbs to the breadcrumbs and mix together. Season each bowlful well.

Dip both sides of the flattened chicken breasts in the flour, then in the egg, then finally in the breadcrumbs.

Heat the oil in a large, shallow frying pan and fry the chicken in two batches. Turn down the heat as soon as one side is golden, continue to cook for a few more minutes, then flip over and cook the other side. To check if the chicken is cooked properly, cut right through the middle. The chicken should be completely white with no hint of pink.

scampi e capesante al cartoccio
prawn and scallop parcels

This dish never fails to get a roar of approval. What I never tell anyone is that it's just about the easiest thing to rustle up in the kitchen.

Prep time: 5 mins
Cooking time: 25 mins

SERVES 4

INGREDIENTS

1 tbsp olive oil, plus extra to drizzle
1 red onion, peeled and finely sliced
½ garlic clove, peeled and crushed
200g cherry tomatoes, halved
½ fennel bulb, chopped, fronds reserved
salt and freshly ground black pepper
400g tagliatelle
200g each scallops and prawns (raw)
1–2 tbsp freshly chopped parsley

Cut four large rectangles of baking parchment about 38 x 50cm each. Preheat the oven to 200°C/180°C fan oven/gas mark 6.

Heat the oil in a pan and fry the onion until softened. Add the garlic and cook for 1 min. Add the cherry tomatoes and the chopped fennel, and cook for 3–4 mins until softened. Season well.

Cook the tagliatelle for 5 mins. Drain well, adding a ladleful of the cooking water to the cherry tomato mixture.

Return the pasta to the pan and add the cherry tomato sauce, season and toss well.

Divide the mixture among the parchment pieces, top each with a quarter of the scallops and prawns. Drizzle over a little oil and sprinkle over the parsley. Fold the parchment into parcels, twisting the ends together so that they stay closed. Put the parcels on a couple of lipped baking sheets and cook in the oven for 20 mins.

Place on plates and serve immediately.

spiedini di pesce
fish kebabs

Simple, quick, eaten in a flash.

Prep time: 10 mins
Cooking time: 5 mins

SERVES 4

INGREDIENTS

4–8 wooden skewers
600g firm white fish, such as pollock,
    cut up into large pieces
2 tbsp mixed herbs, such as oregano
    and thyme
1 garlic clove, peeled and crushed
2 tbsp olive oil
2 tbsp dry white wine
salt and freshly ground black pepper
1–2 lemons, cut into wedges
rocket and tomato salad, to serve

Soak the skewers in cold water for at least an hour.

Pop the fish in a bowl with the herbs, garlic, oil and wine. Season well. Set aside to marinate for 20 mins.

Divide the fish equally among the skewers, finishing with a chunk of lemon, and grill for about 5 mins, turning over halfway through, until the fish is opaque. Serve with the salad.

zucca ripiena al forno
baked, stuffed squash

The versatility of this dish makes it useful. If you serve it on its own, it's good for four people, but if you dish it up alongside the Sunday roast, it could stretch to feeding six or eight (or three to four rugby players). I've used thyme for the herb flavouring, but chopped sage or rosemary would work just as well.

Prep time: 15 mins
Cooking time: 45 mins

SERVES 4

INGREDIENTS

2 small pumpkins or squash
olive oil
salt and freshly ground black pepper
1 medium red onion, peeled and
    finely chopped
2 celery sticks, finely chopped
1 red pepper, finely chopped
a few sprigs of thyme
125g long-grain rice
400ml hot vegetable stock
70g pancetta, cut into cubes
1–2 tbsp freshly chopped parsley
green salad, to serve

Preheat the oven to 200°C/180°C fan/gas mark 6.

Halve the pumpkin or squash lengthways, scoop out the seeds and discard. Put in a shallow roasting tin and drizzle with a little oil. Season and roast for 30–40 mins until just tender.

Heat 1 tbsp olive oil in a pan and fry the onion, celery, red pepper and thyme until softened and golden. Stir in the rice and season, then add the hot stock and cover with a lid. Turn the heat down to low and cook according to the timings on the pack.

Meanwhile, in a separate pan, dry fry the pancetta until golden. Drain well.

When the rice is cooked, stir the pancetta and parsley through it. Remove the pumpkin from the oven, fill with the rice mixture, then return to the oven for 5 mins to warm through. Serve immediately with a green salad.

'Italian food is all about using seasonal ingredients — whatever's fresh at the market that day'

pesce in crosta
fish pie

I love this recipe because you can chuck in whatever fish takes your fancy. Sometimes I mix up white and smoked fish, sometimes I keep it very simple and stick to white fish only. To make it a bit posher, I use salmon and prawns, as I've done here. You can also make the sauce with stock instead of milk, which gives it a slightly lighter feel.

Prep time: 30 mins
Cooking time: about 1 hour

SERVES 4

INGREDIENTS

15g butter
2 shallots, peeled and finely chopped
1 small fennel bulb, chopped
salt and freshly ground black pepper
a splash of vermouth
1 tbsp plain flour
450ml hot fish or vegetable stock
600g mixed fish, such as salmon, halibut
    and prawns
200g frozen peas, thawed
2 tbsp freshly chopped parsley
750g potatoes, sliced to the thickness
    of a £1 coin
2 slices white bread, whizzed into
    breadcrumbs
15g pecorino cheese, freshly grated

Preheat the oven to 200°C/180°C fan oven/gas mark 6.

Melt the butter in a pan and gently fry the shallots and fennel until soft. Season well. Add the vermouth and simmer until the liquid is absorbed by the vegetables.

Stir in the flour and cook for 1 min, then slowly add the hot stock and carry on stirring until all the stock is incorporated into the sauce.

Put the fish and peas into a 1.2-litre ovenproof dish. Stir the parsley into the sauce and season well. Pour the sauce over the fish.

Top with the potatoes, then sprinkle with the breadcrumbs and pecorino. Bake in the oven for 45–50 mins until bubbling and golden and the potatoes are tender. Test them by pushing the point of a sharp knife into them.

Try this wine with it...
Cantine di Monteforte, Pinot Grigio/Chardonnay (Veneto)
White

fagioli all'uccelletto
beans in tomato sauce

Here's our Italian version of baked beans. You need to soak the beans the day before, but that's not a hassle. It's a simple dish to make and it's healthy, student-style grub that everyone loves: cheap, easy and tasty. It'll also keep well in the fridge for three or four days.

Prep time: 10 mins, plus at least
   8 hours soaking
Cooking time: 1 hour 10 mins

SERVES 4

INGREDIENTS

125g dried cannellini or borlotti beans
1 onion, peeled and chopped
1 bay leaf
1 sprig of rosemary
1 tbsp olive oil
1 celery stick, chopped
1 carrot, peeled and chopped
200g can chopped tomatoes
1 vegetable stock cube
salt and freshly ground black pepper
crusty bread and Sacla' Fiery Chilli Pesto,
   to serve

Put the beans in a sealable container and cover with plenty of cold water. Cover with the lid and leave to soak for at least 8 hours.

Drain and rinse the beans, then put them in a pan with the onion, bay leaf and sprig of rosemary. Add 1 litre of cold water and cover. Bring to the boil, reduce the heat, then simmer gently for 1 hour.

When the beans are cooked, heat the oil in a saucepan and sauté the celery and carrot for about 10 mins. Drain the beans and onions, discarding the bay leaf and rosemary sprig, but reserving the cooking liquid, and add the bean mixture to the pan with the celery and carrot. Stir everything together.

Add 200ml of the cooking liquid, the chopped tomatoes and the vegetable stock cube. Stir to dissolve the cube. Season and simmer for about 10 mins until thick and saucy. Serve immediately with bread and the chilli pesto.

Try this wine with it...
Cantine Leonardo da Vinci, Chianti (Tuscany)
Red

linguine alla carbonara
linguine with ham, eggs and cheese

Some people think that cream is essential for this sauce, but it's not. The secret is to cook the pancetta in oil, so there's enough fat in the pan to coat the pasta and mix with the eggy sauce. The amount of Parmesan you add is up to you, so I always put an extra chunk on the table in case anyone wants more. If you can't get hold of pancetta, use streaky bacon instead.

Prep time: 5 mins
Cooking time: 10–15 mins

SERVES 4

INGREDIENTS

400g linguine
2 tbsp olive oil
150g pancetta, cut into small cubes
4 medium eggs
25g freshly grated Parmesan cheese,
    plus extra to serve
salt and freshly ground black pepper

Bring a large pan of salted water to the boil and cook the linguine until al dente.

Heat the oil in a pan and fry the pancetta until golden. In a bowl, whisk the eggs and Parmesan until creamy. Season well.

Drain the pasta and return it to the pan. Add the pancetta plus any oil, and immediately pour in the egg mixture. Stir everything together. Divide among four bowls and serve immediately with lots of freshly ground black pepper and extra Parmesan.

crespoline al prosciutto e ricotta
pancakes with ham and ricotta

These savoury pancakes are a great way of tarting up leftover ingredients. I've used ricotta and ham, but if there are any leftover cooked vegetables in the fridge, bung them in, too.

Prep time: 10 mins
Cooking time: 30 mins

SERVES 4 (2 pancakes per person)

INGREDIENTS
425ml milk
125g plain flour
2 medium eggs
salt and freshly ground black pepper
a little sunflower oil, for frying
500g ricotta cheese
200g ham, chopped
2 tbsp freshly chopped basil
butter, for greasing
300g jar Dallaglio by Sacla'
    Bolognese sauce
freshly grated Parmesan cheese

Put the milk and flour in a bowl and whisk together. Whisk in the eggs and season. Set aside for 20 mins.

Heat the oil in a medium frying pan and ladle in a spoonful of the batter – I'm going to be specific here: you need around 80ml batter per pancake, making a total of eight. Swirl the batter around the pan to cover the base and cook over a medium heat for 2–3 mins until golden. Flip the pancake over and cook the other side. Slide onto a plate and transfer to a warm oven. Repeat until all the batter has been used.

Preheat the oven to 210°C/190°C fan oven/gas mark 6/7.

Mix together the ricotta, ham and basil in a bowl, seasoning well. Divide equally among the pancakes and fold up.

Place the pancakes side by side in a 1.2-litre ovenproof dish greased with butter. Pour the Dallaglio bolognese sauce into a bowl and stir in 50–100ml water to loosen it. Spoon the sauce over the pancakes and sprinkle with grated Parmesan. Bake in the preheated oven for 15–20 mins until heated through.

minestrone del nonno
grandpa's vegetable soup

This time-honoured Italian soup uses whatever vegetables are in season. Start it a day ahead, as the borlotti beans need to be soaked in cold water. My father's finishing touch is crushed garlic mixed with parsley, added at the end.

Prep time: 15 mins, plus overnight soaking
Cooking time: 1 hour 40 mins

SERVES 4

INGREDIENTS

150g dried borlotti beans
1 tbsp olive oil
1 onion, peeled and chopped
1 celery stick, chopped
1 carrot, peeled and chopped
1.2 litres hot vegetable stock
1 potato, peeled and diced
200g can chopped tomatoes
100g green beans, chopped
1 courgette, chopped
100g peas
salt and freshly ground black pepper
50g capelli d'angelo (angel hair spaghetti), broken into pieces
1 garlic clove, peeled
2 tbsp freshly chopped parsley
freshly grated Parmesan cheese, to serve

Put the beans in a large sealable container and cover with double the volume of water. Cover with the lid and leave to soak overnight.

The next day, heat the oil in a pan and fry the onion, celery and carrot for about 5 mins until just softening.

Drain the borlotti beans, discard the water and add the beans to the pan with the hot stock. Cover, bring to the boil, then turn the heat down low and simmer for about 1 hour.

Add the diced potato and cook for a further 30 mins. Add the tomatoes, green beans, courgette and peas and season well. Cook for 5 mins.

Add the pasta and cook for about 4 mins. Meanwhile, chop the garlic and the parsley together and season with a little salt.

Divide the soup between the bowls, then stir in the garlic and parsley mix, and add a little grated Parmesan.

sacla' tip

In place of the garlic and parsley mix, add a dollop of Sacla' Classic Basil Pesto to the minestrone to serve.

spezzatino di pollo
chicken stew with lemon

Chicken thighs suit this dish better than any other part of the bird — they have an earthier flavour than chicken breasts, so they work well with the garlic and lemon. Serve with tagliatelle or your choice of vegetables.

Prep time: 20 mins
Cooking time: 40 mins

SERVES 4

INGREDIENTS

2 tbsp olive oil
1 onion, peeled and roughly chopped
1 tbsp plain flour
salt and freshly ground black pepper
6 skinless, boneless chicken thighs,
    chopped
8 garlic cloves, peeled
½ lemon, chopped
500ml hot chicken stock
2 tbsp freshly chopped parsley

Preheat the oven to 200°C/180°C fan oven/gas mark 6.

Heat the oil in a large, flat sauté pan with lid and cook the onion very gently for about 5 mins.

Put the flour in a shallow dish, season it, then toss the chicken thighs in it. Cook the chicken in batches in the sauté pan with the onion until golden on all sides — it doesn't need to cook through completely.

Tip any remaining seasoned flour into the pan and return the chicken to the pan, along with the garlic cloves and chopped lemon. Pour in the hot stock, cover and bring to the boil. Transfer to the preheated oven and cook for 30 mins until the chicken is tender and the garlic soft. Stir in the parsley and serve.

Try this wine with it...
Midolini, Rosacroce Chardonnay (Friuli Venezia Giulia)
White

lasagne di verdure
vegetable lasagne

The squash family of vegetables make good companion ingredients – cooking enhances their sweetness, but also the flavours of other ingredients that are paired with them. This is good eaten cold the next day, too.

Prep time: 20 mins
Cooking time: 45 mins

SERVES 4–6

INGREDIENTS

15g butter
500g spinach, washed
salt and freshly ground black pepper
nutmeg, for grating
1 tbsp olive oil
1 small onion, peeled and finely chopped
1 red pepper, deseeded and chopped
450g pumpkin or squash, chopped
300g jar Dallaglio by Sacla' Tricolore sauce
a few sprigs of basil leaves, roughly chopped
about 6 dried lasagne sheets
50g mozzarella, chopped
25g freshly grated Parmesan cheese

Preheat the oven to 200°C/180°C fan oven/gas mark 6.

Melt the butter in a very large pan and add the spinach. Cook for a couple of minutes until it wilts down. You might need to do this in two batches. Season with salt and pepper and a little nutmeg.

Heat the oil in a pan and sauté the onion, pepper and pumpkin or squash for about 15 mins, covered with a lid, until softened. The steam will help to cook the vegetables. By the end of this stage, you'll notice that the pumpkin is quite soft and squashy.

Set aside 100g Dallaglio by Sacla' Tricolore sauce, then add the rest to the pan with the basil. Fill the empty jar with cold water and add to the pan. Bring to the boil and bubble for 5 mins until thickened and saucy.

Line a 1.2-litre dish with lasagne sheets, then spoon over a third of the spinach. Cover with a third of the vegetable sauce. Repeat until all the ingredients are used up, then spoon the reserved sauce over the last layer of lasagne. Cover with the mozzarella and sprinkle over the Parmesan.

Cook in the oven for 25 mins until the lasagne is tender and the top is golden and bubbling.

zucchine ripieni
stuffed courgettes

If you want to make the most of courgettes, this is the way to do it. By the way, a quick word about shallots: I've used them in quite a few of the recipes in this book, including this one. That's because they're milder than onions, they have a slightly sweeter flavour, and they also take less time to cook, which is always a good enough reason in our house.

Prep time: 15 mins
Cooking time: 35 mins

SERVES 4

INGREDIENTS
1 tbsp olive oil
4 large shallots, peeled and finely chopped
6 small–medium courgettes,
    halved lengthways
salt and freshly ground black pepper
50g pine nuts
1 tsp thyme leaves
a few sprigs of mint
200ml hot vegetable stock
50g breadcrumbs
25–50g pecorino cheese, grated

Preheat the oven to 200°C/180°C fan oven/gas mark 6.

Heat the oil in a pan and fry the shallots until softened. Using a teaspoon, run down the length of the halved courgettes to hollow them out. Roughly chop these bits and add to the shallots with a drizzle more oil if needed. Season well.

Add the pine nuts to the pan with the thyme and cook for 5–10 mins until softened. Stir in the mint.

Put the halved courgettes in a large ovenproof dish, hollowed-out-side up. Season well, then spoon the cooked mixture down the length of each one. Pour in the hot stock.

Sprinkle with the breadcrumbs and cheese, and cover the dish with foil. Cook in the preheated oven for 20 mins, then uncover and cook for a further 10 mins to brown the top.

Try this wine with it...
Planeta, Cerasuolo di Vittoria (Sicily)
Red

tonno con salsa di pomodoro
tuna with tomato and white wine sauce

As a guy who likes to look after himself, fish is a big favourite of mine. It's a good source of lean protein and vitamin B, and it packs a powerful punch of brain-boosting omega 3. And whether you fry, grill or poach it, it takes less than 30 minutes from pan to plate.

Prep time: 5 mins
Cooking time: 20 mins

SERVES 4

INGREDIENTS

1 tbsp olive oil
1 onion, peeled and finely chopped
2 celery sticks, sliced
100ml white wine
150ml hot fish stock
200g can chopped tomatoes
1 bay leaf
50g pitted black olives
salt and freshly ground black pepper
4 x 150g yellowfin tuna steaks
rocket, to serve

Heat the oil in a wide shallow pan and cook the onion and celery until softened and starting to turn golden.

Add the wine, hot stock, tomatoes and bay leaf, and bring to the boil. Stir in the olives and season. Simmer, covered, for 10 mins.

Lower the tuna steaks into the sauce and cook for about 10 mins – the fish will turn opaque when it's done. Take out the bay leaf, and serve with rocket.

sacla' tip

As an alternative to the tomatoes, bay leaf and black olives, use Sacla' Italian Tomato & Olive Big Bold Italian sauce.

tiella barese
potato and mushroom cheese bake

Here's a heart-warming dish that needs no more than a green salad to go with it. Onions, softened until golden, are stirred together with potatoes and mushrooms, and covered with breadcrumbs and cheese.

Prep time: 10 mins
Cooking time: 40 mins

SERVES 4

INGREDIENTS

1 kg potatoes
2 tbsp olive oil, plus extra for drizzling
1 onion, peeled and sliced
200g chestnut mushrooms, sliced
400ml hot vegetable stock
salt and freshly ground black pepper
2 tbsp freshly chopped thyme
2 tbsp breadcrumbs
2 tbsp freshly grated Parmesan cheese

Peel the potatoes and cut them in half. Put them in a large pan of cold salted water and simmer for 10 mins. Drain and slice into 0.5cm rounds.

Preheat the oven to 180°C/160°C fan/gas mark 4.

Heat the oil in an ovenproof sauté pan and fry the onion until softened. Add the mushrooms and continue to cook until golden.

Slide the potatoes into the pan and toss everything together. Pour over the hot stock, season, and sprinkle with the thyme, breadcrumbs and Parmesan. Drizzle with a little more oil, then cook in the preheated oven for about 30–40 mins until the potatoes are cooked.

'The 1987 Ampleforth 7s team. I'm top left – in those days I played on the wing!'

'It's a dish in itself, but it'll feed a crowd if you serve it with meat or fish'

crema di zucca
butternut squash soup

This silky smooth soup tastes wickedly rich and is really easy to make. When I remember, I double the quantity and freeze half so that there's always some handy for when we're pushed for time.

Prep time: 20 mins
Cooking time: 45 mins

SERVES 4–6

INGREDIENTS

1 tbsp olive oil
1 onion, peeled and finely chopped
1 carrot, peeled and finely chopped
1 celery stick, finely chopped
1 garlic clove, peeled and crushed
1 small butternut squash, peeled and diced
salt and freshly ground black pepper
1 litre hot vegetable stock
1 bay leaf
freshly grated Parmesan cheese

Heat the oil in a pan and add the onion, carrot and celery. Cover and cook over a low heat for 10–15 mins until softened.

Add the garlic and squash, and cook for a few minutes in the softened vegetables. Season well.

Add the hot stock and bay leaf to the pan, season and cover. Bring to the boil, then turn the heat down to a simmer and cook for 20–30 mins until the squash is soft and tender.

Remove and discard the bay leaf. Pour into a blender or food processor and whiz until smooth. Return to the pan, check the seasoning and reheat gently. You may need to add a little more water if the soup is too thick.

Ladle into bowls and grate over a little Parmesan.

sacla' tip

Serve with a generous dollop of Sacla' Classic Basil Pesto.

arancini
risotto balls

Nothing is wasted in the Italian kitchen, so if my grandmother ever had any risotto left over, the next day she'd make it into balls and serve it to us for breakfast. This recipe is a little more refined – when you bite into one, there's a piece of melted mozzarella hidden inside. They're rich, so serve with a rocket salad.

Prep time: 20 mins
Cooking time: 15 mins

SERVES 4

INGREDIENTS
a little orange zest
half the leftover *risotto primavera*
    (see page 66)
a little orange zest
50g mozzarella, roughly chopped
a little plain flour
1 medium egg
salt
5 slices of white bread, whizzed
    into breadcrumbs
sunflower oil, for frying

Mix the orange zest into the risotto. Using a dessert spoon, take spoonfuls of the mixture and push your thumb into the middle to make a small hole. Fill with a piece of mozzarella, then wrap the rest of the risotto around the mozzarella. Continue until you've made all the balls – there should be about 16.

Put the flour in a bowl, beat the egg in another and season, then tip the breadcrumbs into a third bowl.

Coat the risotto balls first in the flour, then toss in the egg, and finally coat with the breadcrumbs.

Pour about 5cm oil into a shallow pan, then fry the balls in batches over a medium heat, until golden all over. Sprinkle with salt before serving.

Try this wine with it...
Cusumano, Nero d'Avola (Sicily)
Red

'Bite into one and you get a delicious surprise of melted mozzarella inside'

pasta con salsiccia
penne with sausage, lemon and cream

It's funny how two or three sausages just slip down, one after the other, but for this recipe even I find that you only need one sausage per person. Choose a good herby banger to give a full and rounded flavour.

Prep time: 20 mins
Cooking time: 30 mins

SERVES 4

INGREDIENTS

1 tbsp olive oil
2 large shallots, peeled and chopped
½ fennel bulb, chopped
1 celery stick, chopped
½ tsp fennel seeds, crushed
4 good-quality sausages
zest of ½ lemon
salt and freshly ground black pepper
50ml double cream
150ml hot chicken or vegetable stock
400g penne
1 tbsp freshly chopped parsley

Bring a large pan of salted water to the boil.

Heat the oil in a pan and sauté the shallots, chopped fennel and celery over a low to medium heat for about 10 mins, until the vegetables start to caramelise.

Stir in the fennel seeds and cook for about 1–2 mins. Slit the skins of the sausages and add the sausagemeat to the pan with the lemon zest. Season well. Use a wooden spoon to break down the meat while it browns.

Pour in the cream and hot stock, then cover and bring to the boil. By this stage, the sausagemeat should have broken down and the mixture should look more like the consistency of a sauce. Simmer for 10–15 mins.

While the sauce is simmering, cook the penne until al dente. Add a ladleful of the cooking water to the sausage sauce, then drain the pasta well. Return the penne to the pan, pour in the sausage sauce, add the chopped parsley and toss everything together. Serve immediately.

calzone
ham and spinach pizza pockets

Calzone means 'trouser leg' in Italian. I'm not sure of the link with pizza dough folded over to look like a Cornish pasty, but nevertheless, the Italians call it *calzone*! I keep the filling simple: Dallaglio Napoletana sauce, spinach and a slice of ham.

Prep time. 30 mins
Cooking time: 15–20 mins

SERVES 4

INGREDIENTS
a little olive oil, for greasing and brushing
1 quantity of pizza dough (see page 72)
a little plain flour, for dusting
300g jar Dallaglio by Sacla' Napoletana
   sauce
100g spinach
4 slices ham
salt and freshly ground black pepper

Preheat the oven to 200°C/180°C fan oven/gas mark 6.

Grease two baking sheets with a little oil. Divide the dough into quarters and roll out one piece into a 22cm round, as if you're making a pizza.

Spread about 1–2 tbsp of the Napoletana sauce over one half of the dough, top with a quarter of the spinach and a piece of ham, and season. Fold the other half on top and curl the edges of the dough round as if you're making a Cornish pasty. Brush with oil and place on the prepared baking sheet. Repeat with the remaining dough and ingredients.

Bake in the oven for 15–20 mins until golden. Warm the remaining sauce in a pan. Put a calzone on each plate, then spoon a little of the warmed sauce over each.

Try this wine with it...
A Mano, Rosato (Puglia)
Rosé

torta rustica
mozzarella, leek and ham pie

As the name suggests, this literally translates as 'rustic tart' – which means you can put whatever you like in it. Don't use too many watery vegetables, though, otherwise the base of the pastry will turn into a soggy mess. You need to bake this pie on a high temperature to start off with, then reduce the heat and cook for a little longer so that the pastry cooks right through.

Prep time: 30 mins
Cooking time: 1 hour 5 mins

SERVES 4

INGREDIENTS
15g butter
2 large leeks, finely chopped
salt and freshly ground black pepper
500g ready-made shortcrust pastry
a little plain flour, for dusting
1 plum tomato, sliced
125g mozzarella
100g ham, roughly chopped
1 medium egg, beaten

Melt the butter in a pan and fry the leeks gently until softened and starting to turn golden. Season well. Transfer into a sieve resting over a bowl to cool.

Preheat the oven to 230°C/210°C fan oven/gas mark 8.

Roll out two-thirds of the pastry on a clean work surface lightly dusted with flour, and line a 20cm round tin with the pastry. Spoon the leeks over the base, top with the tomato slices, mozzarella and ham. Season well.

Roll out the remaining pastry and use it to make a lid. Place it on top, tucking it under the edges of the pastry that forms the bottom of the pie. Fold the edges of the pastry forming the pie bottom over the lid and press down. Prick the lid all over. Brush with the beaten egg and bake in the oven for 20 mins, then reduce the temperature to 170°C/150°C fan oven/gas mark 3 for 35 mins until golden all over.

piatti per occasioni speciali
special occasions

4

Italian food is rarely fussy, but these recipes are for when
we want to mark an event by pushing the boat out
a little more than usual. Often my kids muck in,
and that's when I'm at my most contented.

brasato al barolo
braised beef in barolo

Barolo, the red wine used in this dish, comes from my family's Piedmont region. It's big, powerful and gutsy and is one of my favourite Italian wines. Serve the broth in which it's cooked just as it is with the vegetables, or make into a smooth gravy, as I've suggested here.

Prep time: 20 mins
Cooking time: about 2 hours

SERVES 4

INGREDIENTS
1 tbsp olive oil
1 medium onion, peeled and
   finely chopped
2 celery sticks, finely chopped
2 small carrots, peeled and finely chopped
1 garlic clove, peeled and chopped
1 kg topside of beef
salt and freshly ground black pepper
400ml Barolo wine
bouquet garni (a bay leaf, a few parsley
   stalks, a few sprigs of thyme)
15g butter
1 tbsp plain flour
potatoes and steamed green beans,
   to serve

Heat the oil in a pan, add the onion, celery and carrots and gently cook for 5–10 mins. Add the garlic and cook for 1 min.

Season the beef, then add it to the pan, turning it around until browned and done all over. Add the wine and bouquet garni, cover and bring to a simmer. Cook gently for about 1½–2 hours until tender.

Remove the beef from the pan and set aside on a warmed plate. In a separate pan, melt the butter and stir in the flour. Cook for 1–2 mins until the mixture starts to bubble and has the consistency of a paste. Take the bouquet garni out of the sauce and gradually pour the sauce into the pan with the butter/flour paste, whisking all the time as you go. Bring to the boil and simmer for 5 mins until thickened.

Put a stick blender into the pan and whiz until smooth. Keep warm while you slice the beef. Serve with fried, sliced potatoes and steamed green beans.

Try this wine with it...
Oddero, Barolo (Piedmont)
Red

lasagne con ricotta e castagne
chestnut and ricotta lasagne

There are other recipes in this book that call for ready-made lasagne sheets, but here I've included a recipe for fresh lasagne. It takes me back to summer holidays with my grandparents in Italy, where making the pasta involved the whole family – happy days. It's worth having a go if you have a pasta machine, as it's really not difficult. One shortcut that you might want to try, though, is whizzing the chestnuts in a food processor.

Prep time: 50 mins, plus resting time
   for the pasta
Cooking time: 30 mins

SERVES 4

INGREDIENTS
200g 00 pasta flour
2 large eggs
1 tsp oil
3 shallots, peeled and finely chopped
250g ricotta
250g mascarpone
200g whole chestnuts, finely chopped
1 tbsp each freshly chopped parsley
   and thyme
salt and freshly ground black pepper
nutmeg, for grating
butter, for greasing
25g freshly grated Parmesan cheese

Sift the flour onto a clean board or work surface and crack the eggs into the centre. Use a fork or your (well-scrubbed) fingers to mix together the egg and slowly draw in the flour.

Continue to work the flour in until you make a dough. Knead briefly until soft and sticky. Cover with clingfilm and leave to rest for 20 mins.

Heat the oil in a small pan and fry the shallots gently until softened. Tip into a bowl and allow to cool. When cooled, add the ricotta, mascarpone, chestnuts and herbs, and season well with salt, freshly ground black pepper and a little nutmeg.

Divide the pasta into thirds and roll out each portion thinly, using a pasta machine. Trim to make rectangles to fit a 1.2-litre ovenproof dish.

Preheat the oven to 200°C/180°C fan oven/gas mark 6.

Cook the pasta in boiling salted water for a few minutes, then drain and lay on baking parchment briefly.

Butter the dish, then layer up the pasta and filling alternately, finishing with a layer of pasta. Sprinkle the Parmesan over the top. Bake in the preheated oven for 25 mins until golden and hot all the way through.

porchetta alla romana
roast pork stuffed with herbs

You need loin of pork, not tenderloin, for this recipe. Make sure the meat has a generous covering of skin so there's enough crackling to go round. If you buy it the day before you cook it, take it out of its wrapping and put it in a dish. Dab it all over with a kitchen towel to mop up any moisture from the skin, and put it in the fridge overnight. This helps to make really crisp crackling. Take the meat out about 30 minutes before roasting.

Prep time: 15 mins
Cooking time: about 2 hours

SERVES 4

INGREDIENTS

1 tbsp olive oil
2 shallots, peeled and finely chopped
1 garlic clove, peeled and crushed
1 sprig of rosemary, finely chopped
20g parsley, chopped
a few sprigs of thyme
2 Dallaglio by Sacla' Slow-Baked
   Tomatoes Marinated With Garlic,
   roughly chopped
1.3 kg pork loin, skin scored
salt and freshly ground black pepper

Preheat the oven to its highest setting.

Heat the oil in a pan and fry the shallots for about 10 mins until softened. Stir in the garlic and cook for 1–2 mins.

Tip into a mini food processor and add the herbs and tomatoes. Whiz to make a paste.

Open out the pork and season well. Cut diagonally along the flesh of the pork to make a pocket. Spread the paste inside, then wrap up the pork and tie it with string. Transfer to a roasting tin and rub salt all over the skin. Pour a glass of water into the base.

Roast the joint for 35 mins per 450g, turning down the oven to 190°C/170°C fan oven/gas mark 5 after 25 mins. Check the water every now and then – you may need to add a few glassfuls if it evaporates. When cooked, remove the crackling, slice the pork and serve with crackling and juices from the pan.

gamberi con funghi selvatici
prawns with wild mushrooms

This easy dish has wonderfully clean flavours and it's really quick to knock up.
I stick to the absorption method for cooking rice, as it works perfectly every
time, with every grain distinct and separate.

Prep time: 8 mins
Cooking time: 20 mins

SERVES 4

INGREDIENTS
300g long-grain rice
salt and freshly ground black pepper
1–2 tbsp olive oil
3 shallots, peeled and finely chopped
1 garlic clove, peeled and crushed
splash of white wine
200g wild mushrooms, sliced
400g large raw prawns
1–2 tbsp freshly chopped parsley

Weigh the rice, then put it into a jug so you can see the volume,
and tip it into a pan. The quantity of boiling water you need is
double the volume of rice – for this recipe, that means 650ml,
which you add to the pan with a pinch of salt. Cover, bring to the
boil, then turn the heat right down to low and leave it alone while
it continues to cook, following the timing on the pack.

Heat the oil in a pan and fry the shallots until golden. Add the
garlic and cook for 1 min, then add the wine and allow it to
bubble up in the pan.

Add the mushrooms with another drizzle of oil and cook until
golden. Add the prawns, toss everything together and cook until
the prawns turn pink.

Use a fork to fluff up the rice, then divide among four plates.
Spoon over the prawn mixture, then sprinkle with the parsley
and serve.

pollo alla cacciatora
hunter's chicken

Here's another legendary dish from my father, Vincenzo's, repertoire.
The recipe changes from family to family, but the essential ingredients
remain the same. It's a selection of chicken joints cooked in an onion and
tomato herb sauce. Serve with tagliatelle, polenta or boiled potatoes.

Prep time: 15 mins
Cooking time: 45 mins

SERVES 4–6

INGREDIENTS

1–2 tbsp olive oil
1 onion, peeled and chopped
200g chestnut mushrooms, halved if large
1 garlic clove, peeled and crushed
4 chicken thighs
4 chicken drumsticks
salt and freshly ground black pepper
400g can chopped tomatoes
125ml white wine
a few sprigs of oregano
1 tbsp freshly chopped parsley

Heat the oil in a large sauté pan and fry the onion for about
10 mins until softened. Add the mushrooms and garlic, and
cook until golden. Set aside on a plate.

Add another drizzle of oil, if necessary, and brown the chicken
pieces in the pan, seasoning as you go. Return the onion mixture
to the pan and pour over the tomatoes, wine and 150ml boiling
water. Add the oregano. Cover and simmer for 20 mins until the
chicken is cooked. Sprinkle with parsley before serving.

sacla' tip

If you're in a rush, leave out the garlic, onion and tomatoes.
Instead, fry the mushrooms in the oil, brown the chicken pieces
and then add 400g of Dallaglio by Sacla' Bolognese sauce.
Continue with the recipe from this point.

agnello alla piemontese
leg of lamb with rosemary and garlic

Lamb is one of our favourite Sunday lunch joints. It's rich, so a little goes a long way. I always make gravy out of the juices left in the pan, and I add a teaspoon of redcurrant jelly to it at the end of the cooking to balance the flavours.

Prep time: 20 mins
Cooking time: around 2 hours, plus resting

SERVES 4

INGREDIENTS
2.6 kg leg of lamb
2 sprigs of rosemary
2–3 garlic cloves, peeled and sliced
salt
1 tbsp plain flour
100ml dry white wine
300–400ml hot lamb or chicken stock

Preheat the oven to 220°C/200°C fan oven/gas mark 6.

Using a sharp knife, make a few incisions in the lamb. Snip the rosemary sprigs into a few pieces and pair them up with a slice of garlic. Push them into the incisions, then season all over and put in a large roasting tin. Roast for 20 mins.

Turn down the oven to 190°C/170°C fan oven/gas mark 5 and roast the joint for a further 20 mins per 450g.

Take the lamb out of the oven, transfer it to a plate, cover with foil and leave to rest in a warm place.

Drain off and discard all but about 1 tbsp fat from the roasting tin. Put the tin on the hob over a medium heat and add the flour. Stir until bubbling and mixed in with the fat and juices.

Pour in the wine and allow the mixture to bubble up, stirring all the time. Add the hot stock and bring to the boil. Simmer for about 10 mins until thickened and syrupy.

Taste for seasoning, then pour the juices into a gravy jug and serve with the lamb.

costata alla fiorentina
florentine beef

This dish is celebrated all over Tuscany, not just in Florence. Its secret is its simplicity: when you eat it in a restaurant over there, you get it straight from an open-fire grill. It should be slightly charred on the outside and served either rare or medium rare. You can achieve a similar result at home with a good cast-iron griddle pan. All you need with it is a handful of rocket and some potatoes lightly roasted in olive oil.

Prep time: 5 mins
Cooking time: 20 mins

SERVES 4

INGREDIENTS
2 T-bone steaks
2–3 sprigs of rosemary, chopped
a little olive oil
salt and freshly ground black pepper
1 lemon, cut into wedges

Put the steaks in a shallow container with the rosemary, and drizzle with olive oil. Set aside to marinate for 30 mins at room temperature.

Heat a griddle pan to the point where droplets of water falling on it sizzle and evaporate instantly. Season the steaks and fry, one at a time, for about 5 mins on one side and 3–4 mins on the other. Set aside to rest for 10 mins.

Use a meat knife to carefully slice the meat away from the bone, trim any fat, and slice each piece on the diagonal. Serve with the lemon wedges and an additional seasoning of salt.

sacla' tip
Spoon 4 tbsp Sacla' Classic Pesto over the steak just before you serve it.

bollito misto alla Dallaglio
italian rustic stew

This is my pared-down version of a Piedmontese classic winter dish. If you wanted to cook the traditional recipe, you'd be using ox tongue, veal and beef, which makes enough to feed the entire England rugby team. I've simplified it to chicken and sausage. The sauce that goes with it is a must, as are some plain boiled vegetables alongside, such as potatoes, carrots, baby turnips and onions.

Prep time: 15 mins
Cooking time: 1 hour 15 mins

SERVES 4

INGREDIENTS

1 medium onion, peeled
2 celery sticks
2 carrots, peeled
1 whole chicken
salt and freshly ground black pepper
2 sausages

For the salsa verde

½ garlic clove, peeled
1 tbsp capers
2 anchovies in oil
20g flat-leaf parsley
2 sprigs of basil leaves
1 tbsp white wine vinegar
4–6 tbsp olive oil
salt and freshly ground black pepper

Chop the vegetables into rough chunks and put in a pan. Add the chicken and cover with cold water. Season, cover and bring to the boil. When it has reached a heavy boil, skim away any scum and reduce the heat to a simmer. Half cover the pan at this stage. Cook for 1 hour, then add the sausages and continue to cook for 15 mins.

While the meat is cooking, put all the ingredients for the salsa verde in a mini blender and whiz until smooth. Season well.

Lift the chicken, sausages and vegetables out of the broth, put them on a large platter and keep warm. Bring the liquid up to the boil and simmer until reduced by about a quarter.

Carve the chicken – it'll just fall off the bone – and divide among four plates with some sausage and vegetables. Ladle over some of the broth and serve with the salsa verde sauce.

spigola con pomodori e patate
sea bass roasted with potatoes, tomatoes and olives

This is one of those dishes that you find in many restaurants along the coast of Liguria – the region famous for pesto. It looks impressive and always earns me major brownie points when I serve it up. But, like so much of my cooking, it's actually very simple to knock up. If you have a pan to which everything sticks, then line the bottom with a sheet of baking parchment before you start.

Prep time: 15 mins
Cooking time: 1 hour

SERVES 4

INGREDIENTS

800g potatoes, peeled and sliced
1 large onion, peeled and finely sliced
3 tbsp olive oil
300ml hot fish stock
salt and freshly ground black pepper
2 large sea bass or bream
4 plum tomatoes, halved
a handful of black olives
2 tbsp capers
sprigs of fresh basil

Preheat the oven to 200°C/180°C fan oven/gas mark 6.

Put the potatoes and onion in a large roasting tin. Drizzle with 2 tbsp of the oil and pour over the hot stock. Season well. Roast in the oven for 40 mins.

Slash the fish two or three times on each side, then place on top of the potatoes. Season again. Add the tomatoes, drizzle over the remaining oil and roast for a further 20 mins. Add the olives and capers for the last 5 mins of cooking. The dish is ready when the fish is opaque.

Take out of the oven, sprinkle with the basil and serve immediately.

Try this wine with it...
Ciavolich, Pecorino (Abruzzo)
White

cotechino con lenticchie
sausage with lentils

This is traditionally eaten on New Year's Eve in Italy. It's a great way to feed a crowd because you can make the lentils a couple of days ahead and put them in the fridge, then reheat with a splash of water. Enzo and I love it with good quality pork bangers, but if you can get hold of cotechino sausages from an Italian deli you'll be making the authentic dish.

Prep time: 10 mins
Cooking time: around 30 mins

SERVES 4

INGREDIENTS
1 tbsp olive oil
1 onion, peeled and finely chopped
2 celery sticks, finely chopped
1 carrot, peeled and finely chopped
1 garlic clove, peeled and crushed
200g green or brown lentils
1 bay leaf
650ml hot vegetable stock
1 tomato, chopped
1 tsp balsamic vinegar
8 sausages
2 tbsp freshly chopped parsley

Heat the oil in a large sauté pan and fry the onion, celery and carrot until softened and starting to turn golden. Add the garlic and cook for 1 min.

Add the lentils and bay leaf and stir everything together, then add the hot stock and chopped tomato, and cover and bring to a gentle simmer. Cook for about 20 mins until tender. Stir in the balsamic vinegar.

Fry the sausages in a separate pan. When cooked, serve with the lentils and sprinkle over the parsley.

sacla' tip

For a spicy kick, stir 2 tbsp Dallaglio by Sacla' Diavola pasta sauce into the lentils 5 mins before the end of cooking time.

'Vincenzo, at 28, with his father, Nero (my grandfather), outside the Duomo di Torino in 1962'

stinco di agnello ai funghi
braised lamb shanks with button mushrooms and shallots

Lamb shanks need long, slow cooking, but the result is certainly worth it. They become unbelievably tender and, with this recipe, end up bathed in a fabulously rich sauce.

Prep time: 5 mins
Cooking time: around 2 hours

SERVES 4

INGREDIENTS

1 tbsp olive oil
8 shallots, peeled
1 garlic clove, peeled and crushed
250g button mushrooms
4 lamb shanks
300ml hot chicken or lamb stock
100ml white wine
a sprig of rosemary
salt and freshly ground black pepper
boiled potatoes and steamed
   vegetables, to serve

Heat the oil in a flameproof casserole and fry the shallots for 5–10 mins until starting to turn golden. Add the garlic and cook for 1 min. Add the button mushrooms and cook for 5–10 mins until starting to turn golden, too. Lift out and set aside.

Brown the lamb in the pan. Add the shallot mixture to the lamb, together with the hot stock, wine and rosemary. Season well.

Cover, bring to the boil, then turn the heat down to a simmer and cook for 1–1½ hours, until tender.

Serve with boiled potatoes and steamed veg.

Try this wine with it...
Midolini, Rosacroce Uvaggio Rosso (Friuli)
Red

'Slow cooking means that the meat is so tender it just falls off the bone'

pollo arrosto alla Dallaglio
roast chicken Dallaglio-style

This is roast chicken the Dallaglio way – the difference between this recipe and any other are the ingredients that go into the seasoning. You need sprigs of rosemary and a few garlic cloves, which are stuffed inside the cavity. I mash these into the gravy at the end for added flavour.

Prep time: 5 mins
Cooking time: around 1 hour 20 mins

SERVES 4 with leftovers

INGREDIENTS
1 whole chicken
salt and freshly ground black pepper
2–3 sprigs of rosemary
2–4 garlic cloves (depending on how garlicky you like it), unpeeled
1 tbsp plain flour
200ml dry white wine
400ml hot chicken stock

Preheat the oven to 190°C/170°C fan oven/gas mark 5. Season the chicken cavity and stuff the rosemary and garlic in the cavity.

Put in a roasting tin and season all over. Pour a glass of water into the tin. Roast for 20 mins per 450g, plus an additional 20 mins. It's ready when you stick a skewer into the thigh and the juices run clear. If they're pink, continue to cook, checking every 5 mins.

Take the chicken out of the oven and use a spoon to scoop out the garlic cloves. Put on a warm platter and cover with foil. Set aside to rest. Resting the chicken is important, as it gives the juices a chance to run through the meat, maximising its tenderness by the time you carve it.

Drain and discard all but about 1 tbsp fat from the tin. Stir in the flour and place the tin on a hob over a medium heat. Cook for 1–2 mins until golden and bubbling.

Add the wine, stirring all the while, then pour in the hot stock. Squeeze the soft purée from the garlic cloves into the tin. Mash it into the liquid, stirring it in well. Bring to the boil and simmer until syrupy and thickened. Carve the chicken and serve with the gravy.

lasagne all'emiliana
emilia romagna-style lasagne

I can cook this dish with my eyes shut. It originates in the Emilia Romagna region of northern Italy, where my father was born, and has been handed down through generations of Dallaglios. You need nothing more than a mixed green salad tossed in a simple dressing to go with it.

Prep time: 30 mins
Cooking time: around 1 hour 50 mins

SERVES 4–6

INGREDIENTS
500g lean beef mince
1 onion, peeled and finely chopped
1 carrot, peeled and finely chopped
1 celery stick, finely chopped
400g can chopped tomatoes
1 tbsp tomato purée
300ml hot beef stock
100ml red wine
2 bay leaves
salt and freshly ground black pepper
25g butter
1 tbsp plain flour
400ml skimmed milk
nutmeg, to season
6 dried lasagne sheets
50g freshly grated Parmesan cheese

In a large pan, brown the mince in batches. Use a wooden spoon to press it down and break it up into bits as it starts to colour. Transfer the mince to a bowl. Add the onion, carrot and celery to the pan, and cook for 15 mins until softened and starting to turn golden.

Put the mince back into the pan and add the chopped tomatoes, tomato purée, hot stock, wine and bay leaves. Season well. Cover and bring to the boil, then remove the lid and simmer for 45 mins until the sauce has reduced and thickened.

Meanwhile, melt the butter in a small pan. Stir in the flour and cook for 1 min. Add the milk slowly, stirring all the time to make a sauce. Cook for 1–2 mins until slightly thickened. Season with salt, pepper and nutmeg.

Preheat the oven to 200°C/180°C fan oven/gas mark 6. Put a third of the meat sauce in the bottom of a 1.2-litre ovenproof dish. Top with two lasagne sheets, a third of the white sauce and a third of the cheese.

Repeat the process until all the lasagne sheets and ingredients have been used. Cook in the oven for 30–40 mins until bubbling and golden and heated through.

sacla' tip
If you're short of time, use a jar of Dallaglio by Sacla' Napoletana pasta sauce, plus the same jarful of water again, added to the pan of mince at the end of Step 1, and stir in. Bring to a simmer and cook for 10 mins, then stir in 1 tbsp each freshly chopped parsley and basil. Complete the recipe as above.

pollo arrosto con porcini
chicken stew with porcini mushrooms

In Italy, the traditional name for this recipe is *coniglio arrosto con porcini*, and it calls for rabbit legs (*coniglio* means rabbit). I've used chicken here to broaden the recipe's appeal, but if you want to be traditional, order one jointed rabbit from your local butcher and use all of it. Whichever you use, serve it with polenta or mashed potatoes.

Prep time: 15 mins
Cooking time: 1 hour 5 mins

SERVES 4

INGREDIENTS

20g dried porcini
4 chicken drumsticks and
    4 chicken thighs, skinned
8 rashers streaky bacon
1 tbsp plain flour
salt and freshly ground black pepper
2 tbsp olive oil
4 large shallots, peeled and quartered
1 sprig of rosemary
2 sprigs of thyme
200ml dry white wine

Preheat the oven to 200°C/180°C fan oven/gas mark 6. Put the porcini in a bowl and cover with 150ml boiling water. Set aside.

Wrap the streaky bacon around the chicken drumsticks and thighs, and secure with a cocktail stick. Toss in the flour, then season well.

Heat the oil in a pan and fry the chicken pieces until golden all over. Drain the porcini, reserving the liquid, and add the porcini to the pan with the shallots and herbs. Continue to cook until everything starts to brown.

Season well, pour in the wine and mushroom liquid (strain this through a clean cloth first), then cover with a lid and cook in the oven for 30 mins. After this time, remove the lid and cook for a further 15 mins.

Try this wine with it...
Baiocchi, Sagrantino di Montefalco (Umbria)
Red

merluzzo alla veneziana
venetian salt cod

Start this recipe the day before, because salt cod requires soaking overnight. I've simplified the classic *baccalà alla veneto*, which involves cooking the salt cod with onions and oil until soft and tender. Instead, this recipe involves frying the fish in a little flour and serving it with a drizzle of pesto at the end. The combination of salty cod with creamy, buttery polenta is out of this world. Ask your local fishmonger to get hold of it for you.

Prep time: 15 mins, plus overnight soaking
Cooking time: 30 mins

SERVES 4

INGREDIENTS
500g piece of salt cod
1 tsp salt
300g polenta
1 tbsp olive oil
1 tbsp plain flour
50g salted butter
4 tbsp Sacla' Classic Basil Pesto
½ lemon, cut into 4 wedges

Soak the salt cod overnight in a bowl of cold water. The next day, drain, rinse under cold running water, then cut into four equal pieces.

Put 3 litres of cold water in a pan and bring to the boil. Add the salt and polenta and stir furiously, making sure the polenta doesn't contain any lumps. Reduce the heat and simmer, stirring every now and then, for about 30 mins, making sure the polenta doesn't stick to the pan.

About 15 mins before the end of cooking time, heat the oil in a pan until hot. Toss the salt cod in the flour, then fry it in the pan for about 10 mins, turning halfway through, until golden on each side.

Stir the butter into the polenta and divide among four plates. Top with a piece of fish and drizzle 1 tbsp of pesto over each piece of fish. Serve with a wedge of lemon.

cannelloni con ricotta e funghi
cannelloni with ricotta and mushrooms

Cannelloni tubes look fiddly, but they're actually easy to fill – even for rugby players with hands the size of dinner plates! Use a small teaspoon or a spoon handle to push the filling into each tube. When cooked, cannelloni are firmer than pasta you boil in water – that's because they are baked in the sauce, instead of absorbing loads of water.

Prep time: 20 mins
Cooking time: 35–40 mins

SERVES 4

INGREDIENTS

1 tbsp olive oil
2–3 shallots, peeled and finely chopped
1 garlic clove, peeled and crushed
250g mushrooms, finely chopped
1 tbsp chopped thyme
250g ricotta
salt and freshly ground black pepper
300g jar Dallaglio by Sacla'
    Bolognese sauce
12 cannelloni tubes
2 slices white bread, whizzed into
    breadcrumbs
25g freshly grated Parmesan cheese
green salad, to serve

Heat the oil in a pan and fry the shallots and garlic until softened. Add the mushrooms and thyme and cook until all the juices have been absorbed. Tip into a bowl, cool a little, then mix in the ricotta. Season well.

Preheat the oven to 200°C/180°C fan oven/gas mark 6.

Spoon the Bolognese sauce into a bowl and add 150ml cold water to the jar. Shake to dislodge the bits inside the jar and pour into the sauce. Stir well. Spoon a little into the base of a 1.2-litre ovenproof dish.

Stuff the ricotta mixture equally into the cannelloni tubes. Place in the dish on top of the sauce. Cover with the rest of the tomato sauce. Scatter over the breadcrumbs and cheese, and season. Cook in the oven for 30 mins until golden and bubbling.

Serve with a green salad.

Try this wine with it...
Alpha Zeta, Valpolicella Ripasso (Veneto)
Red

tortelloni di zucca
butternut squash-stuffed pasta

This is the celebratory supper that my grandmother used to give us on Christmas Eve. It makes the most of ingredients that are seasonal in December, with a few store cupboard stalwarts thrown in for good measure. It's a feast that's light, as you don't want to peak too soon when you've got a day of serious eating ahead.

Prep time: 45 mins, plus 20 mins resting time
Cooking time: 40 mins

SERVES 4

INGREDIENTS
600g butternut squash
salt and freshly ground black pepper
200g 00 pasta flour, plus extra for dusting
2 large eggs
4 amaretti biscuits
15g freshly grated Parmesan cheese
nutmeg, for grating
1 egg yolk, beaten
melted butter

'In our house, the men do the Christmas cooking'

Preheat the oven to 200°C/180°C fan oven/gas mark 6.

There's no need to peel the squash, just cut it in half lengthways, scoop out and discard the seeds, then put it in a roasting tin, flat-sides up. Season and roast for 20–30 mins until tender.

Make the pasta dough. Sift the flour onto a clean board or work surface and crack the eggs into the centre. Use a fork or clean fingers to mix together the egg and slowly draw in the flour.

Continue to work the flour in until you make a dough. Knead briefly until soft and sticky. Cover with clingfilm and leave to rest for 20 mins.

Scoop the squash flesh into a bowl, discarding the skin. Crush the amaretti biscuits and stir into the squash with the Parmesan. Season with salt, freshly ground black pepper and a little nutmeg.

Divide the dough into quarters and roll out each piece into long rectangles using a pasta machine. Dust and clean the work surface, and place the first rectangle of pasta on it. Cut it in half widthways to make two smaller rectangles.

Roughly divide the filling into four portions. Then divide each portion into five and place each spoonful, evenly spaced, onto the sheet of pasta. Brush egg yolk around each blob of filling, then gently lay the other piece of pasta on top. Press the pasta down over the filling, making sure there's no air inside. Cut around the blobs to separate each piece. Repeat with the remaining dough to make 20 pieces in total.

Bring a large pan of water to the boil and cook the pasta in batches for a few minutes. Divide among four plates, drizzle with melted butter and grind a little black pepper on top.

Try this wine with it...
Cortegiara, Bardolino (Veneto)
Red

petto di tacchino ripieno
stuffed turkey breast

Christmas Day is a practice run of small courses, building up to the main event: stuffed turkey breast. The important thing here is to season the turkey at each stage; that way you'll get a flavoursome joint. I also use a good, coarse bread – even a seeded brown loaf – to give the stuffing texture. My father, who has been involved with food all his life, makes it an annual habit to remind my kids (and me) to wash hands before and after handling raw poultry to avoid spreading germs around the kitchen.

Prep time: 30 mins
Cooking time: around 2½ hours

SERVES 8

INGREDIENTS

25g butter
1 small onion, peeled and finely chopped
50g sultanas
40g pine nuts
80g country bread, chopped
2 sausages, skinned
leaves pulled from a few sprigs of thyme
a few sprigs of sage, chopped
1 medium egg
a splash of white wine
salt and freshly ground black pepper
100g pancetta
around 3 kg turkey breast
2 tbsp plain flour
200ml dry white wine
600ml hot turkey or chicken stock
1 tbsp redcurrant jelly

Preheat the oven to 200°C/180°C fan oven/gas mark 6.

Melt the butter in a pan and sauté the onion for about 10 mins until softening and turning golden. Stir in the sultanas and pine nuts and cook for 1 min. Tip into a bowl and set aside to cool. Once cooled, add the bread pieces, sausages, herbs and egg, and mix together. Moisten with a splash of wine and season well. Mix again.

Lay the pancetta on a chopping board, each slice slightly overlapping the other. Place the turkey breast on top, skin-side down. Use a knife to cut into the turkey flesh along the length of it to create a pocket. Season well and push the stuffing evenly into the pocket, then replace the turkey flap to cover.

Cut five or six lengths of string long enough to go round the turkey. Slip them under and along the width of the turkey, and tie tightly to keep everything together. Flip over, place on a plate and weigh. Calculate the cooking time and roast for 15 mins per 450g, plus 15 mins. Put in the roasting tin and pour a glass of water into the base, cover with foil and roast in the oven. Keep topping up the water every 20 mins or so. Remove the foil 20 mins before the end for the pancetta to brown nicely.

To test if it's cooked all the way through, insert a skewer into the thickest part of the joint and check the juices run clear. If not, continue to cook, checking every 5 mins.

Put on a warm plate, cover with foil and set aside. Drain and discard all but 1 tbsp fat from the roasting tin. Add the flour to the tin and place over a medium heat. Stir it into the juices and cook for 1–2 mins until it's bubbling and looks paste-like. Pour in the wine, stirring all the time, then gradually stir in the hot stock. Add the redcurrant jelly. Bring to a simmer for about 5–10 mins until thickened and syrupy. Taste to check the seasoning. Pour the gravy into a warm jug and serve with the turkey.

dolci sensazionali
sensational desserts

5

It's hard to imagine a brute like me making delicate fillings for pastry confections, but a good pud is a work of art that delights the senses. Increasingly, though, the kids bag making that part of the meal.

cioccolata calda
hot chocolate

Here's a twist on two highly addictive items: hot chocolate and chocolate puddings. It needs to be served as soon as you spoon it into the bowls, so it's a make-between-courses pud – but as long as you have everything prepared, it will only take a few minutes.

Prep time: 15 mins
Cooking time: 5 mins

SERVES 4

INGREDIENTS

100ml double cream
2 tsp icing sugar
250g dark chocolate, broken into pieces
4 tbsp rice flour
200ml milk
2–3 tbsp caster sugar
1 tbsp amaretto liqueur
2 amaretti biscuits, crushed

Whisk the double cream with the icing sugar until soft and mousse-like. Chill.

Put the chocolate pieces in a pan and pour over 100ml cold water. Melt the chocolate over a medium heat.

Add the rice flour and use a wooden spoon to mix all the ingredients together, stirring all the time, until thickened – it won't take long.

Slowly add the milk, caster sugar and liqueur, and whisk constantly until smooth and thick. Spoon into four 150ml ramekins, top with a dollop of chilled whisked cream and a sprinkling of amaretti biscuits, and serve immediately.

affogato al caffè
ice cream with espresso

You could be forgiven for thinking that with a list of just two ingredients, who needs a recipe? *Affogato al caffè* translates as 'drowned with coffee', but it's the way the 'drowning' is balanced that makes or breaks this dessert. Too much coffee and the ice cream melts into a mess; too little and you'll just have a revoltingly sweet dessert. This balance is just right.

Prep time: 5 mins

SERVES 4

INGREDIENTS
a tub of vanilla ice cream
200ml hot espresso coffee

Scoop the vanilla ice cream into balls and put one or two scoops each into four small bowls that have been chilled in the freezer first.

Pour 50ml of coffee into each of four espresso cups and let everyone drown their own ice cream!

panna cotta ai frutti di bosco
traditional Italian cream pudding

This recipe is very rich, so even I reckon that a little goes a long way. I use less gelatine than in most recipes, because I like a softer texture when it's set. Serve with a tumble of berries in summer, or poached plums in winter.

Preparation and cooking time:
30 mins, plus overnight chilling

SERVES 4

INGREDIENTS
3g gelatine leaves
200ml double cream
200ml full-fat milk
1 vanilla pod, split lengthways
75g golden caster sugar
summer berries, such as raspberries,
    blueberries and strawberries, to serve

Soak the gelatine in a small bowl of cold water.

Put the double cream, milk and vanilla pod in a pan and bring just to the boil. Turn off the heat and leave to infuse for 30 mins.

Add the sugar and stir to dissolve. Lift the gelatine out of the water and add it to the cream. Stir to melt, then strain the mixture through a sieve and into a jug.

Pour among four 110ml ramekins, or dariole moulds if you have them. Cover and chill overnight.

Dip each mould briefly into a bowl of boiling water, then carefully run a knife around the inside to dislodge the contents. Turn onto plates and scatter over the berries. Enjoy.

torta al limone
lemon tart

You can cheat and buy a ready-made lemon tart, but there's nothing to beat a homemade one – especially this one. Besides, it's Alice's all-time favourite, so my share price rises sharply every time I produce it.

Prep time: 30 mins, plus 40 mins chilling
Cooking time: 1 hour 20 mins

SERVES 10–12

INGREDIENTS

1 quantity sweet pastry (see page 187), chilled for 20 mins
4 medium eggs
175g golden caster sugar
175ml double cream
zest and juice of 3 lemons
icing sugar, to dust

Preheat the oven to 200°C/180°C fan oven/gas mark 6.

Roll out the pastry and use it to line a deep 23cm fluted round tart tin (see my tips on the Apple and frangipane tart recipe on page 187). Cover with a piece of baking parchment and chill for 20 mins.

Fill the covered pastry with baking beans (you can use rice or uncooked dried beans, too) and bake in the oven for 15–20 mins until dry to the touch. Remove the beans and the baking parchment, and continue to cook for 5–10 mins until completely dry. Turn down the oven to 150°C/130°C fan oven/gas mark 2.

In a bowl, mix together the eggs, sugar and double cream. Stir in the lemon zest and juice – you'll notice the mixture thicken: that's the acid combining with the cream. Pour into the pastry case and bake for 50 mins until just set. Leave to cool in the tin.

Remove the tart from the tin, dust with icing sugar, then slice and serve.

Try this wine with it...
Pieropan, 'Le Colombare' Recioto di Soave (Veneto)
Sweet white

zabaglione
frothy italian custard

This classic boozy dessert is said to have originated in Piedmont. The heat holds the egg yolks, sugar and wine together, so as soon as it's whisked, don't delay getting it to the table, as it needs to be eaten straightaway.

Prep time: 20 mins

SERVES 4

INGREDIENTS
3 medium egg yolks
40g golden caster sugar
125ml Marsala wine
Italian biscuits or langue de chat, to serve

Put the egg yolks, sugar and wine together in a large glass bowl. Rest over a pan of simmering water, making very sure that the base doesn't touch the water.

Whisk the ingredients together until the mixture forms soft peaks and the texture is mousse-like.

Spoon into four individual glasses and serve with the biscuits.

'The egginess almost persuades me that zabaglione is mainly about protein...'

torta con nocciole e cioccolato
chocolate and hazelnut cake

This cake involves chopped, toasted hazelnuts in a rich chocolate sponge. Eat it any way you like – either as an afternoon pick-me-up, or as a pud with a dollop of mascarpone. Chop the nuts in a food processor, if you like, but don't over-whiz them or they'll turn greasy and the cake will be heavy.

Prep time: 20 mins
Cooking time: 40–50 mins

SERVES 10

INGREDIENTS

125g unsalted butter, chopped,
   plus extra for greasing
100g blanched hazelnuts
150g dark chocolate (minimum 70%
   cocoa solids), broken into pieces
4 medium eggs
150g golden caster sugar
50g plain flour
1 tsp baking powder
mascarpone and cocoa powder, to serve

Grease and line a 20cm loose-bottomed round cake tin with baking parchment. Preheat the oven to 180°C/160°C fan oven/gas mark 4.

Toast the hazelnuts in a dry frying pan until golden. You'll know when they're ready, as there'll be an amazing aroma of roasted nuts driving your taste buds crazy. Finely chop them.

Put the chocolate in a bowl and melt over a pan of simmering water, making sure the base doesn't touch the water. Don't touch the chocolate until it has all melted, otherwise it can 'seize' and thicken.

Add the chopped butter to the bowl and allow it to melt in slowly, then stir. Remove the bowl from the heat and set aside to cool.

Whisk the eggs and sugar in a bowl for about 5 mins until soft and mousse-like in texture. Fold the chocolate into the mixture, then the chopped nuts, flour and baking powder.

Spoon the mixture into the tin and bake for 40–50 mins, until the top of the cake feels firm when pressed. Remove from the tin onto a plate. Cool a little, then slice, and serve with a dollop of mascarpone and a dusting of cocoa powder.

'My daughter, Josie, is a total chocaholic —
she press-ganged her brother and sister
into helping to make their mum a birthday
cake. Pretty good effort'

zuccotto toscano
frozen tuscan dessert

This dessert originated in Tuscany and is one of those brilliant recipes that needs very little expertise, but makes you look terrific. Buy whole, candied peel and chop it yourself. You'll find it at the supermarket in boxes of lime, lemon and orange. Choose whichever flavour floats your boat.

Prep time: 20 mins, plus overnight freezing

SERVES 6–8

INGREDIENTS

240g plain sponge cake
juice of 1 large orange
2 tbsp brandy
150ml double cream
1 tbsp icing sugar, plus extra to dust
25g dark chocolate, grated
60g glacé cherries, chopped
40g candied peel, finely chopped

Line an 800ml pudding basin with clingfilm to make it easier to turn out the contents at the end.

Slice the cake and use it to line the sides and base of the pudding basin, making sure every bit of the bowl is covered. Keep a little bit of cake left over to cover the filling.

In a bowl, mix together the orange juice and brandy, and spoon all over the sponge.

In a separate bowl, beat the double cream and icing sugar together until thick enough to just hold its shape. Fold in the chocolate, cherries and candied peel, and spoon the mixture into the basin and level. Cover with the remaining slices of sponge cake, then cover with clingfilm. Freeze for at least 8 hours.

Remove the pudding from the freezer and turn out onto a plate. Take off the clingfilm and dust with icing sugar before serving.

'A Dallaglio joint venture — making pancakes in the Farinet Hotel kitchen in Verbier, 2008'

biscotti all'arancia e nocciole
hazelnut and orange biscuits

These biscuits are traditionally enjoyed at the end of the meal with a glass of Vin Santo – Italian dessert wine. You can buy them in any deli, but making them is a cinch and they keep for ages in an airtight container. I like the hazelnuts with skins on, as they give more flavour.

Prep time: 10 mins
Cooking time: 1 hour, plus 10 mins
   cooling

MAKES ABOUT 32 BISCOTTI

INGREDIENTS
2 medium eggs
225g granulated sugar
80g hazelnuts
50g unsalted butter, melted
1 tsp baking powder
zest of 1 orange
325–350g plain flour

Preheat the oven to 190°C/170°C fan oven/gas mark 5.

Whisk the eggs and sugar together in a large bowl or in the bowl of a mixer until pale, thick and mousse-like – this will take about 5 mins. Fold in the hazelnuts, melted butter, baking powder, orange zest and enough flour to make a smooth, slightly sticky dough. Bring together with your hands and knead roughly on a board.

Split the dough in half and shape it into two long, flat rectangles about 23 x 7cm each. Place them on a baking sheet lined with baking parchment and bake for 20 mins.

Take out of the oven and allow to cool on the baking sheet for 10 mins. Line another baking sheet with baking parchment.

Reduce the oven temperature to 150°C/130°C fan oven/gas mark 2. Slice each long piece of baked dough on the diagonal into 1.5cm slices. Lay the slices flat on a baking sheet and bake for a further 40 mins, turning over every 10 mins until cooked through and pale golden. Leave to cool on the baking sheets, then pack into airtight containers and store for up to a month.

macedonia di frutta
fruit salad with cinnamon and spice

This sweetly spicy syrup turns a fruit salad into an occasion, and makes it a favourite in the Dallaglio household in winter.

Prep time: 15 mins
Cooking time: 5 mins

SERVES 4

INGREDIENTS
50g golden caster sugar
juice of ½ orange
1 cinnamon stick
1 kg fruit, such as apples, oranges, grapes,
    mango, kiwi fruit and pineapple

Put the sugar in a pan with the orange juice and cinnamon stick. Add 100ml cold water. Bring to the boil and simmer for about 3–4 mins until the sugar has dissolved and the liquid is syrupy. Allow to cool.

Prepare the fruit: slice the apples and segment the oranges and put them in a large bowl. Cut the grapes in half, if you like, and chop the mango into chunks. Peel and chop the kiwi fruit and pineapple.

Pour the syrup over the fruit and leave to macerate for a couple of hours before serving.

semifreddo alla vaniglia
speedy vanilla ice cream

No need for an ice-cream machine to make this lighter-than-air confection – just whisk all the ingredients together. We flavour it simply with vanilla and serve it with a selection of sliced fruit.

Prep time: 20 mins, plus chilling and freezing

SERVES 8

INGREDIENTS
1 vanilla pod
600ml double cream
4 medium eggs, separated
125g golden caster sugar

Slit the vanilla pod in half lengthways, then run the rounded end of a table knife along the length of each half to scrape out the seeds. Transfer to a small bowl.

In a separate large bowl, whip the double cream until thick and moussey. Fold in the vanilla seeds, then chill in the fridge.

Whisk the egg whites in a clean, grease-free bowl until stiff peaks form. Add 1 large spoonful of the sugar and whisk it in. Set aside.

In a separate bowl, whisk the egg yolks with the remaining sugar until doubled in size. Next, fold the chilled cream into the egg yolk and sugar mixture until they are combined.

Fold a large spoonful of the beaten egg whites into the mixture until mixed in, then fold in the remainder.

Spoon the mixture into a sealable container and freeze for at least 8 hours.

pere cotte nel vino rosso
pears cooked in red wine

This dessert couldn't be easier and, best of all, you can make it up to three or four days in advance. Make sure you turn the pears every 10 minutes or so, so that all sides get poached evenly in the wine.

Prep time: 15 mins
Cooking time: 45 mins

SERVES 4

INGREDIENTS
4 pears
300ml red wine
75g golden caster sugar
pared zest of ½ orange
1 cinnamon stick, broken

Peel the pears, leaving the stalks intact, and use a sharp knife to remove the calyx at the base.

Put the red wine in a medium pan, big enough for the pears to fit snugly in the base, with the sugar, orange zest and cinnamon stick. Add 100ml cold water. Heat gently to dissolve the sugar.

Add the pears, cover with a piece of scrunched up greaseproof paper and cover with a lid. Covering the pears with greaseproof paper will create steam within the pan, which will poach the pears beautifully.

Bring to the boil, then reduce the heat to low and cook for 45 mins, tossing the pears halfway through. Lift out of the pan and put each on a dessert plate. The liquid will have reduced to a fantastic syrup – divide this among the pears and serve immediately.

torta di polenta con arancia
orange and polenta cake

No baked pudding captures the spirit of Italy more than the ones that include polenta and are flavoured with oranges. Polenta is yellow cornmeal, and it can be coarsely or finely ground. Here, you need the fine type so that the texture isn't gritty. This pud is a big hit at home.

Prep time: 20 mins
Cooking time: 45 mins

SERVES 10

INGREDIENTS
175g unsalted butter, plus extra
   for greasing
3 oranges
200g unrefined caster sugar
3 medium eggs, beaten
200g self-raising flour
50g fine polenta

Grease and line the base of a 22cm round cake tin with baking parchment.

Slice two of the oranges thinly (you'll need enough slices to cover the base of the tin, so one and a half oranges may be enough). Put the slices in a large pan with 150ml water. Bring to the boil and simmer for a few minutes to poach.

Lift out the orange slices and place them in the base of the tin. Add 2 tbsp of the sugar to the liquid in the pan and bring to the boil. Simmer until the liquid is syrupy and reduced by half. Pour the syrup into the prepared tin over the orange slices.

Preheat the oven to 190°C/170°C fan oven/gas mark 5.

Zest the remaining orange and squeeze to extract the juice. Put the butter and remaining sugar in a bowl and cream together until light, pale and fluffy. Gradually add the beaten eggs, then fold in the flour with the orange zest, juice and polenta. Mix everything together.

Spoon the mixture into the tin and level. Bake for 35 mins or until a skewer inserted into the centre comes out clean. Cool in the tin for 10 mins, then tip the cake out onto a plate, cut into slices and serve with vanilla ice cream (see page 175).

'There's nothing incongruous about
a former rugby player baking!'

tiramisù
'pick me up' pud

'Pick me up' is the literal translation of *tiramisù* and you can see why, given the caffeine in the espresso and cocoa. Add to these two ingredients sweet mascarpone mousse, sponge biscuits and Marsala wine, and it's pretty wicked, even as desserts go.

Prep time: 15 mins, plus chilling

SERVES 6

INGREDIENTS

3 large eggs, separated
75g icing sugar
300g mascarpone
100ml espresso or strong black coffee,
    cooled
2 tbsp Marsala wine or rum
18–20 Savoiardi biscuits (sponge fingers)
cocoa powder or dark chocolate
    (minimum 70% cocoa solids)

In a bowl, whisk the egg yolks, icing sugar and mascarpone together until combined.

In a separate clean, grease-free bowl, whisk the egg whites until stiff peaks form. Fold one spoonful of the egg whites into the mascarpone mixture to loosen, then gently fold in the remainder.

Put the coffee and Marsala in a shallow bowl. Dip half the Savoiardi biscuits into the coffee liquid and line a 1.2 litre serving dish with the soaked biscuits. Spoon over half the mascarpone mousse.

Repeat with the remaining biscuits, dipping them in the coffee, and finish with a layer of mascarpone mousse. Dust with cocoa powder or finely grate a little dark chocolate over the top.

Chill for at least a couple of hours to set, then remove from the fridge 30 mins before serving.

torta di formaggio con limone
lemon cheesecake

Although biscuit-based cheesecakes are the norm here, the sponge-based, European style is the one I prefer. If life's too short to make it from scratch, buy a ready-made sponge flan case and use the base of the tin as a template to cut out a circle. Alice is crazy about lemony puddings, so ours tend to get eaten as soon as they come out of the oven, but they're best if they chill overnight, as the flavours come together and the texture becomes firm and creamy.

Prep time: 20 mins
Cooking time: 1 hour, plus overnight chilling

SERVES 12

INGREDIENTS
For the base
10g unsalted butter, melted,
    plus extra for greasing
1 medium egg, at room temperature
50g golden caster sugar
zest of ½ lemon
50g self-raising flour

For the topping
600g full-fat cream cheese
100g golden caster sugar
3 large eggs, separated
zest of 2 lemons
½ tsp vanilla extract
juice of 1 lemon

Grease and line a 20cm round spring-form cake tin with baking parchment. Preheat the oven to 160°C/140°C fan oven/gas mark 3.

Make the sponge base. Whisk the egg and sugar together in a bowl until soft and frothy and the mixture leaves a ribbon-like trail.

Add the lemon zest, flour and melted butter, and gently fold all the ingredients together. Bake in the oven for 15 mins until the cake is golden and 'squeaks' slightly when pressed on top. Leave to cool.

To make the topping, beat together the cream cheese, sugar, egg yolks, lemon zest, vanilla extract and lemon juice.

In a clean, grease-free bowl whisk the egg whites until stiff peaks form. Fold 1 tbsp into the cream cheese mixture, then add the remaining egg whites and gently fold everything together.

Pour into the prepared tin, on top of the sponge, and bake for around 45 mins. Cool in the tin, then chill overnight before serving. Remove from the fridge 30–60 mins before serving to allow the cheesecake to reach room temperature.

crostata di more e prugne
plum and blackberry crumble with amaretti

This is a fruity concoction that uses the best late-summer fruit and is an ideal sweet ending for Sunday lunch. Once your oven is free after cooking the roast, put the crumble in and it'll be ready when you've finished eating the main course. To make it slightly healthier, you can swap half the flour for wholemeal flour. Serve with ice cream, a drizzle of double cream or custard.

Prep time: 15 mins
Cooking time: 40 mins

SERVES 6

INGREDIENTS
For the fruit
9 plums, halved and stoned
225g blackberries
2 tbsp light muscovado sugar
1 tsp ground cinnamon
½ tsp ground ginger
juice of ½ orange

For the topping
175g plain flour
125g unsalted butter, chilled and cubed
50g amaretti biscuits, crushed
25g flaked almonds
25g light muscovado sugar

Preheat the oven to 200°C/180°C fan oven/gas mark 6.

Put the plums and blackberries in a large bowl. Add the sugar, spices and orange juice, and toss everything together. Spoon into a 27 x 20cm shallow ovenproof dish.

Sift the flour into a large bowl. Add the butter and rub in roughly – there should still be a few clumps of butter. Stir in the crushed amaretti biscuits, flaked almonds and sugar.

Spoon the topping evenly over the fruit and bake in the oven for 40 mins.

sorbetto all'arancia
orange sorbet

This is a zingy and refreshing, palate-cleansing sorbet. If you leave out the egg white and rough it up with a fork, you get the other classic Italian ice, granita.

Prep time: 20 mins, plus freezing

SERVES 4

INGREDIENTS
6 large oranges
150g golden caster sugar
1 medium egg white

Zest two of the oranges and set the zest aside.

Use a sharp knife to cut away the peel and pith from all the oranges, revealing the orange segments. Cut in between each section of orange skin to remove the segments.

Put the segments in a blender and whiz to make juice. Pour into a jug – you should have 600ml liquid.

Put the juice in a pan with the sugar and heat gently to dissolve the sugar. Pour into a sealable freezer-proof container, and cool. Freeze for a couple of hours until firm and crystallised, but not frozen solid.

Scoop out the frozen juice and put in a blender again with the egg white. Whiz to combine. Pour back into the container and freeze until solid.

'Orange sorbet is summer on a plate — an echo of my long school holidays spent in Italy'

crostata di marzapane alle mele
apple and frangipane tart with pine nuts

You can buy sweet pastry, but my kids like to make it. You have to blind-bake the pastry first (bake it first on its own, without the filling), otherwise its base won't cook and will end up soggy. The finished dessert is stunning, but it's very rich, so serve it in thin slices with a spoonful of thick cream.

Prep time: 30 mins, plus 40 mins chilling
Cooking time: 1 hour 20 mins

SERVES 10–12

INGREDIENTS
For the sweet pastry
200g plain flour, plus extra for rolling out
100g chilled unsalted butter, diced
1 medium egg yolk

For the filling
350g cooking apples, peeled, cored
  and chopped
2 tsp golden caster sugar
1 tsp plain flour
a good pinch of ground cinnamon
150g unsalted butter, softened
150g golden caster sugar
1 medium egg
1 tbsp plain flour
150g ground almonds
50g pine nuts

Start by making the pastry. Put the flour in a food processor and add the butter. Whiz until it feels like sand. In a small bowl, mix the egg yolk with 1 tbsp water and pour in. Whiz again until the mixture forms slightly bigger clumps. It should still look crumbly.

Tip into a bowl and bring together with your hands, kneading lightly to make a soft dough. Shape into a disk, wrap in clingfilm and chill for 20 mins.

Roll out the pastry on a lightly floured board or clean work surface. Use it to line a deep, 23cm fluted flan tin. Cover with a piece of baking parchment and chill for 20 mins. Preheat the oven to 180°C/160°C fan oven/gas mark 4.

Fill the parchment-lined tin with baking beans (you can use rice or uncooked dried beans, too) and bake for 15–20 mins until dry to the touch. Remove the beans and baking parchment, and continue to cook for 5–10 mins until completely dry.

Toss the apples, sugar, tsp flour and cinnamon together in a bowl, and scatter over the base of the pastry.

Beat the butter and sugar together in a bowl until soft and creamy, then beat in the egg. Fold in the tbsp flour and ground almonds.

Spread over the apples to cover – a palette knife is ideal for pushing the mixture down. Scatter with the pine nuts and bake in the oven at the same temperature for 50 mins. If the pine nuts look like they're going to burn, cover with a sheet of foil.

Cool the tart in the tin until either warm or completely cold, and serve with thick cream.

Try this wine with it...
Deltetto, Arneis Passito 'Bric Liun' (Piedmont)
Sweet white

index

Buon appetito!

Sun-ripened tomatoes, fragrant sweet basil, pungent onions, celery, garlic, herbs and olive oil – these form the basis of Italian cooking. Simplicity is the key: the sun concentrates flavours, so top-quality, fresh ingredients harvested at the peak of their perfection don't need much help in delivering a big flavour punch. This is what defines the Sacla' philosophy.

Dallaglio collection

This is the range that Dad and I produced with Sacla'. We took a long time in our own kitchen and then at the development kitchens at Sacla' in Italy, and we're very proud of what we've achieved. We hope you enjoy cooking with them as much as we enjoyed creating them.

DALLAGLIO BY SACLA' DIAVOLA

'Diavola' means 'little devil', and this certainly qualifies. Fiery red chillies and garlic combine with vine-ripened tomatoes in an Italian classic.

DALLAGLIO BY SACLA' TRICOLORE

Soft and creamy mozzarella, sweet vine-ripened tomatoes and fragrant basil – a true Italian sauce that's perfect for pasta.

DALLAGLIO BY SACLA' BOLOGNESE

Onions, carrots and celery mingle with tomatoes and herbs, infused with a generous glug of local Barbera red wine.

DALLAGLIO BY SACLA' NAPOLETANA

Fresh-tasting, chopped tomatoes and basil combined with onion, carrot and celery – wonderful stirred through pasta, or as a base for something more complicated.

DALLAGLIO BY SACLA' ITALIAN SLOW-BAKED TOMATOES MARINATED WITH CHILLI

Italian plum tomatoes peeled, oven-baked and marinated in oil and piquant chilli. Fabulous on pizza, sandwiches or in any tomato-rich sauce.

DALLAGLIO BY SACLA' ITALIAN SLOW-BAKED TOMATOES MARINATED WITH GARLIC

Rich and succulent tomatoes, slowly baked, then marinated in oil and tangy garlic and capers, rich in vitamins and antioxidants.

Sacla' collection

Italian food without basil, Sacla' pesto's key ingredient, is unthinkable. Herbs are central to the nation's cooking, but among them, basil is king. There are over 20 varieties, but sweet basil is the one most commonly used in the Italian kitchen: with its pungency and distinctive aroma, released the moment you brush its leaves, for me it's synonymous with everything that is glorious about Italian food. Sacla' produce many sauces, but these are the ones I can't do without in our kitchen...

SACLA' CLASSIC BASIL PESTO

An aroma of freshly picked basil, the rich release of crushed pine kernels and a hit of newly grated Grana Padano cheese.

SACLA' SUN-DRIED TOMATO PESTO

Fragrant basil, sun-dried tomatoes, Grana Padano cheese and, as with all great pesto sauces, crushed pine kernels. Mellow, but intense.

SACLA' ORGANIC TOMATO PESTO

A vivid blend of organically nurtured, aromatic basil, sun-dried tomatoes, extra virgin olive oil and crushed pine kernels.

SACLA' ARTICHOKE ANTIPASTO

Tender and irresistible quarters of Italian globe artichokes, traditionally prepared with flat-leaf parsley in clear, golden oil.

SACLA' TOMATO & OLIVE BIG BOLD ITALIAN SAUCE

Italian tomatoes and olives left to become plump and ripe in the glorious Mediterranean sunshine, in a robust, chunky stir-through sauce.

Acknowledgements

This book could not have happened without the help and support of so many people. Enormous thanks are due to Hilary Ivory and Nigel Wright, who as editor and art director, made our words and ideas come alive; to home economist Emma Marsden who, assisted by Charlotte Dunne, had the job of testing all our recipes and making sure that our measurements and cooking times were accurate; to Ruth Jenkinson, for capturing the most beautiful pictures of my family in action in the kitchen, around the table, and in the garden; to Steve Baxter for his absolutely stunning food photography; and to my assistant, Rachel Bayes, for keeping my life organised and on track.

I'm also grateful to the Ercole family at Sacla' in Italy, who make our sauces and, of course, to Clare Blampied, the Managing Director of Sacla' UK, and her team, who work tirelessly to promote our Dallaglio by Sacla' sauce range. Thanks, too, to my publishers, Simon & Schuster UK and, in particular, editorial director, Francine Lawrence, who not only believed that a rugby player can also cook real food, but helped me produce the book I wanted.

Of course, the people who deserve the greatest thanks are my family. My father, Vincenzo, for having the patience, time and energy to educate me from an early age on everything he knew about food and wine. And for what stability there is in my life, I must thank my beautiful wife, Alice, and our three amazing children, Ella, Josie and Enzo.

Finally, I dedicate this book to the memory of my sister, Francesca, whose last conversation with me was at the table sharing a family meal on the night she died; and also to my late mother, Eileen, who supported me every step of the way and who gave me the unshakable belief that it wasn't just okay to shoot for the moon, it was essential.

Photos not taken specifically for the book are by Sim Canetty-Clarke (wedding picture of Alice and me), Getty Images (me playing rugby), and from the Dallaglio and Ercole family albums.